A CONCISE HISTORY OF
Ancient Greece
to the close of the Classical era

PETER GREEN

*with 208 illustrations
and 6 maps*

BOOK CLUB ASSOCIATES
LONDON

This edition published 1973 by
Book Club Associates
By arrangement with Thames and Hudson Ltd

Printed and bound in Great Britain by
Jarrold and Sons Ltd, Norwich

A CONCISE HISTORY OF

Ancient Greece

Contents

Preface and Acknowledgments

This book had its original genesis in a survey course on ancient Greek history which I gave between 1966 and 1971 at College Year in Athens, and a similar course on the intellectual history of Greece delivered in my capacity as Visiting Professor of Classics at the University of Texas (1971–72). I would like to express my thanks to all those students and colleagues whose critical interest in my lectures helped to make them less inadequate than they might otherwise have been: and to the Librarians of the American School of Classical Studies in Athens, and the Department of Classics in the University of Texas, under whose kindly and ever-helpful auspices my text took final shape. But my greatest debt, as always, is to Greece itself: my home for nine years, my inspiration for a lifetime. If I have reached any understanding of ancient Greece, it is the modern, and perennial, Greek genius I have to thank for it. To my friends in Athens and elsewhere, then, this inadequate *quid pro quo*, in return for untold kindness and illumination, from a more than grateful metic.

Austin, Texas
December 1972   Peter Green

From stone to iron: the prehistoric period

Introduction: sources of knowledge

The Greeks have influenced Western society more, and more fundamentally, than any other nation known to history. Not even Judaism has exerted so perennial and vitalizing an impact on later ages, let alone in so many spheres: reaching beyond faith and morals to the whole complex of literature, philosophy, science and aesthetics. Greek ideas, Greek art and architecture, even (to a surprising extent) Greek language, are all with us today. So is the Greek ideal of democracy, having undergone various odd sea-changes, and more often – now as then – honoured in the breach than the observance. Numberless banks, colleges and town halls still display formal devices (columns, dentils, pediments) first employed by the Greeks. (Architects who are tired of being reminded that such features lack a true context may take comfort from the fact that Greek stone temples were themselves artificial to a degree, being faithfully imitated from a functional structure in wood.) The legacy and fermentation of Greek culture, in fact, long outlasted the real history of ancient Greece.

When did that history begin? A century ago such a question was easily answered. Scientific progress might have cast doubts on Archbishop Ussher's claim that God created the world in 4004 B C; but the statutes of Oxford University firmly pegged the beginning of Greek history to 776 B C, the traditional date for the foundation of the Olympic Games. This is not so arbitrary as it sounds. Winners in the Games (held every four years, this period being known as an 'Olympiad') had their names recorded, and the resultant list provided the Greeks with some sort of common chronological guide-line. About the same time, or a little later, writing – based now on a true alphabet rather than a syllabary – became sufficiently widespread to

1 Opposite: south-east gallery of the citadel of Tiryns, in the Argolid (late thirteenth century BC). Later Greeks, believing that such walls must have been built by giants, were responsible for the term 'Cyclopean' still used to describe them by archaeologists. The blocks are so huge that the outer ones in the upper course merely 'lean in' to form a vault.

2 Detail of Linear A script on a clay tablet from Hagia Triada in southern Crete: Late Minoan I (1570–1400 BC). This script replaced hieroglyphics on Crete c. 1750 BC, and in turn gave way to Linear B c. 1450. It has not yet been deciphered, nor is there agreement as to the language in which it was written.

serve the needs, not only of official scribes and recorders, but also of traders, businessmen and poets. The mid eighth century, in fact, marks that great watershed between prehistory and history proper, between the silent testimony of archaeological exploration and the voice of written evidence. It is astonishing how much light even the Linear B tablets shed on Knossos and Pylos, though their style (as Sherlock Holmes remarked of Bradshaw's railway timetable) is terse, but limited – about as eloquent, in fact, as a laundry-list.

Before Homer and Hesiod, to put it bluntly, we lack the entire intellectual framework of Greek society, and the far-ranging archaeological discoveries made during the past hundred years should never obscure this central truth. We shall see in a moment what *can* be filled in by the archaeologist: but first, a reminder of what can not. Unless we count the oldest layer, the *Ur*-stratum, in Homer and other accounts of the traditional myths, we have no literature whatsoever to illuminate either Crete or Mycenae. Oddly, this is not true for some other Near East civilizations. Fifteen hundred years and more before Homer, the Sumerian epic of Gilgamesh speaks out loud and clear:

'There is no permanence. Do we build a house to stand for ever, do we seal a contract to hold for all time? Do brothers divide an inheritance to keep for ever, does the flood-time of rivers endure? It is only the nymph of the dragon-fly who sheds her larva and sees the sun in his glory. From the days of old there is no permanence. The sleeping and the dead, how alike they are, they are like a painted death. What is there between the master and the servant when both have fulfilled their doom?' (Sandars, p. 104.)

Here is something for which there is no substitute in stone or clay:

3 Detail of a Mycenaean amphora with Linear B script (fourteenth century BC). This script was introduced *c.* 1450 BC, and turns up at Pylos as late as 1200. The late Michael Ventris deciphered it, and found he had to do with a species of proto-Greek. But, from the material studied, it looks as though Linear B was originally designed to express a language other than Greek.

the living word, the human spirit. It is hard, similarly, to visualize the men behind the Hittite or Assyrian bas-reliefs until we study the correspondence in the royal archives, and a third dimension suddenly emerges. Who would have guessed, from the archaeological record, that a Hittite emperor was capable of ending his letter to the King of Ahhijawa (Achaea): 'I suggest that the fault [for our differences] may lie not with ourselves but with our messengers; let us bring them to trial, cut off their heads, mutilate their bodies, and live henceforth in perfect friendship' (Page, p. 12)? And who, in the last resort, could ever have deduced the *Iliad* from a Dipylon vase?

On the other hand, our perspective of early Greek culture has lengthened immeasurably in recent years. The process began during the nineteenth century, when Schliemann – impervious to scholarly scepticism and hostility – revealed the buried treasures of Troy and Mycenae, while Sir Arthur Evans dug his way into the very labyrinth of Knossos – though he rather spoilt the effect afterwards by restoring it in late Victorian Art Nouveau. The refinement of technique evolved by later archaeologists would have astonished Schliemann, who had his own rough-and-ready, not to say brutal, way of dealing with a site. It should not astonish us. In such a work as this too little attention tends to be paid to the actual evidence, whether artefact or document, the foundations on which both history and prehistory rest. Lack of space demands concision; but historical method is at least as important (and indeed illuminating) as historical narrative, and should never be neglected, even in a general survey. This seems an appropriate point to outline the main archaeological, linguistic and scientific techniques that have been developed with a view to interpreting our ever-increasing mass of prehistoric evidence, in Greece as

4 Artefacts from Saliagos (*see* pl. 5); (*a*) a long-bladed tool of obsidian, a glassy black volcanic stone mostly found on Melos, and capable of being worked to a fine edge; (*b*) sherds of burnished pottery bearing white-painted decoration; (*c*) a restored pot.

elsewhere. In the south-west Peloponnese alone, according to recent reports, about fifty Middle Helladic and over a hundred Late Helladic sites have now been surveyed; and this list is by no means exhaustive. Such excavations are proceeding all over the Balkan peninsula. How do we evaluate the material evidence they offer?

There is, first and foremost, all the human detritus which turns up on any populated site: the pottery, more or less indestructible, with its varieties of shape, function, decorative pattern and style; the tools and instruments (*e.g.* spades, axes, hoes, needles, saws) which reveal specialized interests; the presence and absence, and type, of weapons and fortifications; house-building techniques, the placing of sites. Above all, and embracing each of these elements, there is the archaeological technique of stratification by layers, digging precisely through to each successive section and thus laying bare a chronological record in reverse. On Neolithic sites the method has, within recent years, been refined to an extraordinary degree. Inch-thin layers are sliced off, and in each the soil discolorations are precisely charted.

By superimposing all these separate surveys on a master-chart, and analysing the changes in matter, not only earthen foundations but post-holes and wattle (which leave traces of decomposed wood) can be outlined in detail. Stratification can also reveal certain historical changes, more often than not disastrous. For example, the archaeologist will tell you, 'if the fifth stratum above virgin soil contains a widespread layer of ash and the sixth a new style of weapon, house-foundation, and pottery, one may conclude that the pottery underwent a critical change at this point'. And the people too, one might add: such a record forcibly suggests that invaders attacked them, burnt their homes, and largely replaced them. (Total genocide or expulsion, however, is rare: the indigenous population may submerge, but seldom vanishes altogether.) Several parallel and coeval stratified sites imply a common civilization, such as that we find, with modifications, all over the Aegean from the Bronze Age onwards, known variously as Cycladic (the Aegean islands), Minoan (Crete) and Helladic (the Greek mainland). Such cultures, as we shall see (pp. 26 ff., 37), are

5 The site of Neolithic Saliagos, a tiny islet off Antiparos in the Cyclades. Today it rises less than 16 ft above sea-level; it takes its name from a land-snail which likes thorny vegetation. This Middle to Late Neolithic Cycladic culture is quite distinct from that of the mainland or Crete.

loosely divisible into chronological periods, though their dating is by no means uniform (*e.g.* the Neolithic, Bronze and Iron Ages begin at different times in different areas).

We can make some external chronological checks from the comparatively precise records kept by Hittite, Babylonian and Egyptian priests. These, being mathematically based, provide us with dates of an accuracy unobtainable in Greece: king-lists, for instance, assignable in terms of our own calendar. The Egyptian Pharaoh Amenhotep III reigned 1412–1376 B C; seals and scarabs of his consort Queen Tiy have been found in Crete at the Late Minoan (LM) II level, and also at Mycenae among material of Late Helladic (LH) III. As the former ends, and the latter begins, about 1400, we can peg this date – with other corroborative evidence, which rules out the possibility of these artefacts being antiques – as the median transitional period.

Linguistic studies, too, if properly interpreted, can tell us a good deal about tribal movements and indigenous population layers. Greek belongs to the widespread Indo-European family of languages, and was first brought to the Balkans (though probably not in any form which we would readily recognize) between 2100 and 1900 B C (*see* pp. 37–8) by successive waves of invaders from beyond the Danube and the Black Sea area. The loan-words these newcomers borrowed from the local population – vine, olive, fig, wheat and the sea, among others – suggest very clearly that they were pastoral high-landers from the inland steppes. They had no term for a bath-tub: that too is significant. Such clues, like the later distribution of local Greek dialects, can provide us with a useful pattern; but just what such a pattern means in specifically historical or political terms is less certain. Conquest? Racial fusion? Commercial penetration? Without a written record how can we be confident of distinguishing between them? The effective boundaries between one dialect and another must always have been shifting: to treat a dialect area as a clearly defined political or geographical unit can lead to serious misconceptions.

The best fixed criteria for significant change in the population of any given area are still new burial customs, changes in house style, tools, pottery and weapons, or the appearance (detectable by cranio-metry) of a new physical type. Scientific aids such as the Carbon-14 test, which measures the dissipation-rate of radio-activity, can help in dating early artefacts, but the possible margin of error in conducting the test itself still remains uncomfortably wide. Climate and geography – discussed more fully below – can also provide a check on movements, since primitive peoples disliked moving from one climatic zone to another, on the grounds that this disrupted their traditional economy. Thus migrations (*see* pp. 46–7) tended to be horizontal (*i.e.* E–W or

W–E) rather than vertical (N–S or S–N), and to keep roughly the same height above sea-level, except in very unusual circumstances. Mycenaeans, Phoenicians and Greeks alike tended to colonize only the coastal fringes, and to leave the hinterland alone, especially when – as in Anatolia – it was mountainous plateau.

Lastly we have the retrospective tradition, both oral and written, of myth and legend. This is enormously valuable, but at the same time has to be handled with the sharpest and most cautious critical acumen. The epic poets and mythographers embroidered and slanted much of their material, misunderstood more, and got a great deal plain wrong; but as often as not there turns out to be a solid substratum of fact underlying their fancies. The Trojan and Theban cycles, for example, both seem to contain a solid core of genealogical and narrative truth. Archaeologists are busy digging up Thebes' seven gates, while numerous Near Eastern finds in that neighbourhood (including cylinder-seals) suggest that the story of Cadmus and the Phoenician alphabet may likewise rest on relatively firm historical tradition. We should not underestimate the tenacity of oral memory, which tends to

6 Opposite: marble Cycladic doll, *c.* 2000 BC. These delightful figurines – either standing, as here, or squatting (the latter known as 'fiddle idols' because of their resemblance to a violin) – continued to be produced through most of the third millennium BC.

7 Terracotta model representing a scene of sacrifice to the dead, from Kamilári, near Phaestos, Crete. Such a find, coupled with the attention bestowed on Cretan burials, suggests a belief in the after-life. The couples with tables of offerings in front of them may be the deceased themselves, or perhaps chthonian (underworld) deities.

be lost with the advent of writing. The Trojan Expedition in Homer belongs very largely to a half-misunderstood Bronze Age, even though the similes are drawn from Homer's own eighth-century Ionia. How much of Agamemnon's world, though, would we guess at from the technically much 'harder' evidence of the Linear B tablets? In the beginning was the Word: without written records, our account of any civilization, however intuitive and sympathetic, must inevitably remain what T. S. Eliot called 'hints and guesses, hints followed by guesses'. In the last resort perhaps that is true, to some extent, of all historiography.

Climate and geography

The author of that oddly named treatise *On Airs, Waters and Places* (perhaps Hippocrates himself, certainly a Hippocratic physician writing in the late fifth century B C) reveals, long before Montesquieu, a very clear awareness of environmental influence. 'The people of Europe', he writes (meaning, of course, Greece), 'differ from one another both in stature and in shape, because of . . . severe heat waves, severe winters, copious rains and then long droughts, and winds, causing many changes of various kinds' [§23]. These factors, he asserts, lead to 'wildness, unsociability, and spirit'. To call the Mediterranean climate of Greece 'temperate', as people sometimes do, is highly misleading. It ranges between extremes of heat and cold, with violent winds (most noticeable on the islands) in winter and summer alike. During July and August the whole Aegean is scoured by a dominant north-east gale known in antiquity as the 'Etesian Winds', and today as the *meltemi*. Autumn and spring rains tend to be brief but torrential. The effect of these seasonal deluges on rivers, combined with the mountainous, deforested nature of the landscape, is to produce torrents which are either dry-bouldered or in spate, and either way completely non-navigable. Snow is common in the mountains, and can lie on peaks like Parnassus or Olympus as late as June.

The combination of summer drought, winter rains and long spells of winter sunshine is ideal for long-germinating plants such as the fig, vine and olive, which between them sum up the basic core of Mediterranean farming. For a country so dependent on wheat and barley as a staple cereal, Greece is surprisingly ill-adapted to large-scale arable farming. Its soil, except in the plains, is thin, and less than one-fifth of the whole Greek land-mass is, or was ever, cultivable. This had a profound effect on the country's political and economic history, since from a comparatively early date much of its wheat (and timber) had to be imported from unreliable sources abroad. On the other hand, because of its dry, clear air, Greece suffered remarkably few epidemics in comparison with other European countries, and those

which did occur (*e.g.* the great plague during the Peloponnesian War: *see* pp. 136–7) tended to be brought about by extraneous causes. Malaria was largely confined to low, marshy areas like central Boeotia, where the anopheles mosquito could breed. Since Greece is traversed by high mountain ranges, movement in winter tended to be minimal: storms at sea and snow-bound passes kept all but the most persistent travellers at home. War, therefore, tended to be a seasonal affair. There were exceptions to this rule; but between November and February, for the most part, winter quarters prevailed.

For so small an area Greece offers considerable climatic variations. The northern part of the country, including Macedonia and Thrace, is not Mediterranean at all, but lies on the main Continental shelf. The west coast is wetter, and warmer in winter; optimum Mediterranean conditions are found in Attica, and on the Aegean islands. One sharp climatic distinction, not dependent on latitude, is that between mountain regions and littoral. The result, during antiquity, was a social gap: coastal settlements tended to be more developed, while the hinterland remained backward. Differences were – and still are – accentuated by the tree-belt level. Above three thousand feet the Greek uplands provide summer pasturage (in those areas where deforestation has not left a wilderness of barren limestone). One or two states, such as Sparta, possessed both valley and upland territory

8 Aerial view of Mount Olympus, the highest mountain in Greece (9,573 ft) and traditionally the home of the Olympian deities. This gigantic massif, lying on the borders of Thessaly and Macedonia, acted as a bulwark against invaders from the north, though it could, with effort, be circumvented.

suitable for grazing; but most were restricted to either one or the other – Attica and Corinth, for instance, are more or less all lowland, while Arcadia forms a great mountain plateau – and this made a great difference to their economy and social outlook. The only extensive low-level pasturage was in Boeotia and Thessaly: no wonder that from prehistoric times (as the great cattle-pound of Gla, by Lake Copais, eloquently testifies) these areas formed the home of rich and aristocratic cattle-barons, who could breed horses and afford a cavalry arm in battle. Chariots, too, were restricted to the plains, and not merely on grounds of expense: Greek mountain trails, in antiquity as today, could be negotiated by nothing more complex than pedestrians and pack-animals. Wherever possible, the Greek preferred to ship his goods from harbour to harbour along the coast.

Another marked effect of Greek climate is on social life. Weather can be bad: talking of February Hesiod says, with good reason: 'Beware of the month Lenaion, bad days, that would take the skin off an ox.' But trouble is, for the most part, limited to a three-day blow,

9, 10, 11 Different in so many respects, the cultures of Crete and Helladic Greece reveal a common dependence on sheep and (to a lesser degree in Crete) cattle. Below: a unique offering from Middle Minoan East Crete (Palaikastro): a votive bowl containing over two hundred model sheep, and their shepherd. Opposite: the general setting looking east (above) and the Acropolis (below) of Gla in Boeotia – a cattle-baron's stronghold with ample pasturage round Lake Copais.

12 Detail from a black steatite rhyton shaped like an ostrich-egg, known (for obvious reasons) as the 'Harvester Vase', and found in the villa of Hagia Triada, Crete (*c.* 1550 BC). The flails and sickles suggest an olive-harvest; the tinkling of the sistrum and the cheerful singing hint at inebriation; in either case the relief technique is superb.

and winter seldom closes in as it does in northern Europe. Apart from a few grim weeks when men huddle over games of *tric-trac* in stuffy, smoke-filled cafés (as formerly they gathered round the fire of the blacksmith's forge), life in Greece is, to a remarkable degree, conducted out of doors. Three hundred days of sunshine per annum fostered a predominantly verbal (rather than literary or reflective) culture. Public argument eclipsed private research. Poetry was for public recitation; the forensic speech made more impact than the political pamphlet. All the main characteristics of the fifth-century (and indeed the modern) Greek can be detected here in embryo: the verbal alertness, the passion for argument, the trigger-happy temper, the towering pride, the prickly sense of honour, the need to save face at all costs. And all this on a bare – though healthy and vitamin-rich – diet: stone-ground bread, goat's cheese, a handful of olives and figs, diluted wine, a little honey, some eggs and dried fish, with meat a rarity, to be eaten only on feast-days (fat and bones kept for the gods) or some other special occasion.

The Balkan peninsula is not a natural appendage either of Europe or of Asia. Modern political considerations have obliterated the true unit, both social and geographical, which is the Aegean basin: a sea-filled coastal circle including Greece, Crete, the islands and the west coast of Asia Minor from Caria to the Hellespont (Dardanelles).

This all forms part of the great curving range of the Dinaric Alps, calcareous limestone moulded into older crystalline rocks, their quartz giving the same strange amethyst glow from Hymettus by Athens or Mycale on the mainland opposite Samos. This mountain range, known in northern Greece as the Pindus, is reinforced by a number of transverse outcrops on its eastern side: Parnes, Othrys, Ossa, Olympus, forming natural barriers between Attica and Boeotia, Thessaly and Macedonia. These mountains were not so great a deterrent to travel as is sometimes alleged, but they did tend, throughout Greece, to create independent cantons, each (more often than not) with a triple slice of mountain, plain and coast. Hence the social polarization into three close-knit and often antagonistic groups – herdsmen; farmers; fisher-folk and traders – which we encounter in early Athenian history (*see* p. 88). (One main route, however, was always open for invaders: down the east coast from Macedonia, by Thermopylae and the Cithaeron massif into Attica.) In both north and south – the latter especially – plains were few, small (nothing over ten to twelve miles long or five to eight miles wide), and politically important: the Megarid, Marathon, Lake Copais, Messenia, the Eurotas Valley. The larger ones tended to produce reactionary governments based on stock-breeding, with a built-in risk of social agitation (Messenian serfs, Spartan Helots) in more developed periods.

13 Detail from painted stone sarcophagus, Hagia Triada (*c.* 1450–1400 BC). Two herds-men wearing leather skirts or aprons carry calves (or deer, as the dapples suggest) to sacrifice. Priest and altar are to their right, but not shown here.

Greece presents a long and vastly indented coastline, with a plethora of islands and numerous deep fjords: nearly 2,000 miles of it, in fact, for only 31,504 square miles of territory. A redundant coast-line tends to produce social cohesion, and to keep littoral and hinter-land divided: coast-men against plain-men, plain-men against hill-men, with those in the mountains pressing down into the arable zone, the farmers encroaching on the coastal strip, the fisherfolk and traders fighting back, then finally emigrating. Fjords and numerous islands also encourage maritime trade, if not navigational know-how. Unlike the Phoenicians, Greek sailors hardly ever lost sight of land, and when they did they regarded it as an unmitigated disaster, preferring to make short hauls from one island to the next and beach their craft at night, thus dispensing with the need for astro-navigation or dead reckoning. Oddly, for a country where it is hard to get more than forty miles from the sea, which in any case provided them with all their main communication routes, the Greeks were poor and generally reluctant sailors. Who, after all, except in the direst emergency, would dream of voyaging with Odysseus?

The breaking up of the land into a series of isolated cantons tended (in classical antiquity, though not at other periods) to produce small, self-sufficient states, with a proud tradition of social and political independence. It also encouraged that twin curse of *polis* civilization, creeping parochialism and small-town bloody-mindedness, plus occasional delusions of grandeur, as when the Spartans sent an admonitory message to the Great King of Persia ('Who *are* the Spartans?' Darius asked, on reading it). The lack of good roads may profitably be contrasted with both Italy and Asia Minor, where excellent communication systems made for large empires; as we might expect, all the most notable city-states in Greek history – Argos, Sparta, Athens, Thebes – were attached to plains. Since rivers were seldom navigable, and then only for limited seasons, sea-traffic became doubly important, and the control of key straits and isthmuses (the Hellespont and Bosporus, the Isthmus of Corinth, the Straits of Messina) a frequent *casus belli* during the historical period.

Partly through a lack of natural resources, partly because of ruthless and self-defeating depredations by man, Greece very soon ceased to be economically self-supporting. Even by Solon's day (*c*. 570 BC) she had begun to feel the pinch. With a rising population, and a shortage of good alluvial soil, there was little hope of growing enough wheat to satisfy home consumption. The natural trend was to seek grain abroad and turn from subsistence farming to an import-export economy: hence the interest which Athens, in particular, took in wheat-growing areas abroad: south Russia, Egypt, Sicily. And climate plus geography set up a further acute problem: timber shortage. Constant ruthless over-felling for shipbuilding and charcoal (the only true fuel known to the Greeks) depleted the forests, while the ubiquitous domestic goat ate up the young seedlings before they could reach maturity. The result was deforestation, which in turn led to soil erosion, as tons of top-soil – that rich *terra rossa* which, under present climatic conditions, will not re-form once removed – were brought down by the seasonal rains. Plato in the *Critias* paints a horrifying picture of the degree to which this process had advanced even by his day, in the fourth century B C. Here was a political as well as an economic problem, since the flourishing fleet on which fifth-century Athens depended for her livelihood demanded vast and constant supplies of lumber – all, now, to be imported. To make matters worse, though Greece had superb potter's clay and marble, the country was fundamentally deficient in minerals. There was iron in Spartan Laconia; and Athens' silver-mine at Laurium, it is not too much to say, altered the whole course of her history. A remarkable proportion of Greek (especially Athenian) foreign policy was dictated by the perennial need to secure grain, timber or precious metals in an area where natural resources were always inadequate.

14 Entrance to one of the many mining-shafts at Laurium, in South Attica near Cape Sunium. Though sporadic surface mining had been practised since the Iron Age, it was not until Peisistratus' day (sixth century BC) that systematic exploitation of the ore-layers began, culminating in the rich strike at Maroneia (483 BC) which paid for the fleet with which Athens helped defeat Xerxes, and floated those four-drachma silver coins known as 'Attic owls' (*cf.* pl. 54). The mines were leased to contractors and worked by slaves and condemned criminals; the galleries averaged 3–4 ft in height only, so that miners had to operate prone, supine or on hands and knees.

15 General map of Ancient
Greece and the Aegean.

THRACE

Hebrus

BLACK SEA

Pangaeus
Eion

Thracian
Bosphorus

Perinthus   Byzantium
                                Chalcedon

BITHYNIA

PROPONTIS

THRACIAN SEA

Thasos
Samo-
thrace

Imbros

Athos

Aenus

Cardia
Sestos   Lampsacus   Cyzicus
Abydos

TROAD   PHRYGIA

Sigeum   Troy

Ida

MYSIA

Lemnos

caicus

Methymna   Perga-
                                mium

AEGEAN SEA

Mytilene
Lesbos

Arginusae Is.

Phocaea   Hermus

PHRYGIA

Sardis

Clazo-
menae

LYDIA

Magnesia

Chios   Smyrna

IONIA

Colophon

BOEOTIA

Marathon

Andros

Tenos

Samos

Ephesus   Magnesia   Maeander

Celaenae

PAM-
PHYLIA

Miletus   CARIA

Syros

Mykonos

Icaria

CYCLADES
Paros   Naxos

Halicarnassus

LYCIA

Melos

Ios

Amorgos

Thera   Astypalaea

Rhodes
Rhodes

Lindos

CRETAN SEA

Carpathos

Casos

Knossos

Crete
Ida   Dikte   Kato Zakro

Phaestos

| 0 | 20 | 40 | 60 | 80 | 100 Mls |
| 0 | 20 | 40 | 60 | 80 | 100 | 120 | 140 | 160 Kms |

16 Wild goat (*agrimi*) standing on rock, detail from an
egg-shaped stone rhyton, one
of the most remarkable finds
unearthed at the newly (1961)
discovered Minoan Palace of
Kato Zakro in East Crete.
This palace was built during
the sixteenth and early fifteenth
centuries BC, and probably
overwhelmed by the same earthquake (?1500 or 1450) that
destroyed the other major
Cretan palaces.

Minoan Crete

Today, paradoxically, we know far more about Minoan Crete – and
indeed about Bronze Age Greece in general – than the Greeks of the
classical period ever did. For them, the break between Knossos and
the world which later (*c.* 800 B C) emerged from the Dark Ages was
total, and that between Mycenae and the *polis* (city-state) very nearly
so. The myths provided a tenuous link: Talus the brazen giant,
Theseus and the slaying of the Minotaur. Plato in his *Timaeus* seems
to have picked up a garbled reminiscence of the Cretan thalassocracy
(which Solon allegedly got at third-hand from the priests of Egypt,
perhaps retranslating their name for Crete as 'Atlantis'). Homer's
Phaeacians are uncommonly like Sir Arthur Evans's Minoans; and
the Homeric dancing-floor which 'Daedalus made for Ariadne in
broad Knossos' has now been laid bare by the spade for the delectation
of tourists. The high and marvellous Cretan civilization, with its bull-
vaulting and its al fresco religious ceremonies, its topless priestesses
and its parabolic drains, its unplanned agglutinative architecture, its
hedonistic gaiety and colourful frescoes, its elegant indifference to the
military virtues, vanished, after about half a millennium of existence
(*c.* 2000–1400 B C), as though it had never been, leaving only the
haziest tradition behind. Its rediscovery forms one of archaeology's
most striking (and most undeniably romantic) achievements. It also
tends to generate strong emotional reactions. Minoan culture reveals
features as modern as they are anti-classical: these have an immediate
appeal for a generation which has coined the slogan 'Make love not
war', while they have profoundly irritated most puritans and military
activists.

Until about 1500 B C the history of Crete can be treated separately
from that of the mainland. One obvious reason for the island's
isolated development is its size. At 160 miles long, with an area of
3,200 square miles, lying like a horizontal bar between Greece and
Africa, Crete forms a self-supporting and independent world,
economic no less than geographical. Its south coast is protected by
sheer cliffs and unpredictable seas, and it has several fine natural
harbours along its northern shore. The easiest approach by sea is from
the east, along that string of islands – Kasos, Karpathos, Rhodes –
which once formed a land-bridge to Anatolia. By this route (perhaps
as early as 6000 B C, though continuous habitation can only be traced
from the middle of the fifth millennium) the first true Cretans came,
paddling their high-prowed dugout canoes. They settled mostly in
the eastern part of the island, though deep Neolithic deposits suggest
that Knossos, too, was occupied. About 2500 this Stone Age group
received a sporadic (and peaceful) influx of metal-working
immigrants, also from Anatolia.

The settlers led a comfortable, uneventful existence. Fine climatic conditions encouraged them to live in the numerous limestone caves with which Crete abounds. All crops grow well on the island, and the mountains were then still thickly forested, with plentiful wild game for the hunter. Sheep, goats and possibly cattle were raised domestically. (The famous *agrimi*, or Cretan wild goat, still survives in the remoter parts of the White Mountains.) Cretan farmers cultivated the olive, stored their grain in huge earthenware jars and by 2300 were sufficiently prosperous and civilized to build such wealthy private villas as the red-stuccoed 'House on the Hill' at Vassiliki, just south of Gournia. It is not, however, until after 2000 B C, when the island's political and economic centre of gravity shifts to the two central palace sites of Knossos and Phaestos, that Crete gives any real hint of that astonishing phenomenon known as the 'Palace Civilization'. As time went on, these centres acquired more and more power, and evolved a high artistic culture unlike anything on the mainland. We can, in fact, glimpse the outline of an urban revolution taking place, though its details must necessarily remain obscure. Widespread trade, based on a powerful fleet, brought steadily increasing affluence. The needs of commerce, and their own native brilliance, led the Cretans through all the main pre-alphabetic systems of writing in a staggeringly short time, moving on from

17 Landscape near Phaestos and Hagia Triada, looking north towards the Ida mountain range. The wilder parts of Crete have changed little over the centuries, though the hunter's gun has driven the *agrimi* to ever-remoter fastnesses.

pictograms to hieroglyphs and finally to an advanced syllabary (Linear A). A palace bureaucracy grew up and flourished. The introduction of the potter's wheel produced a whole range of exquisite ceramics (*e.g.* the so-called 'Kamares Ware', with its flowing decorative motifs based on natural forms). Unwalled cities reveal an absence of wars or invasions – in sharp contrast to the situation on the mainland.

This peaceful evolution, the so-called 'Pax Minoica', was probably organized by a loose confederation of rich, aristocratic clans, doing well out of an expanding economy, and moving steadily towards a centralized empire based on Knossos (ruled by a theocratic priest-king whom later generations remembered as 'Minos', a term perhaps equivalent to the Egyptian 'Pharaoh'). It coincides with the building (*c.* 2000–*c.* 1700 BC) of the early palaces, and the establishment of roads and guard-posts all over the island. About 1730 a great earthquake – Knossos lies across a seismic fault – shook down most of the existing palaces, at Phaestos and Mallia as well as at Knossos. These were subsequently rebuilt, on the same rambling, agglutinative principles as before, but far more sumptuously, expanding outwards from a great central court in a warren of workshops, storage magazines and luxurious private apartments. (During the sixteenth century at least one new palace emerged, that of Kato Zakro, on the eastern tip of the island.) Cretan culture reached its peak in the three centuries

18 Storage jars (*pithoi*) in the West Block of the Palace at Knossos. These *pithoi* were often big enough to take a man inside; their average capacity ranged upward of forty gallons, and they were used to preserve grain, dried vegetables, wine, oil or honey. Note the ritual 'horns of consecration' in the background.

19, 20 Above left: view of the West Front of the Palace at Phaestos. From Phaestos also (*c.* 1800 BC) comes the Kamares Ware jug (above).

21 View of the Palace at Kato Zakro, Crete, from the north slope across the main excavation. Over 70 rooms have been excavated to date: the total count is probably 250–300, covering an area of about two acres.

29

between 1750 and 1450: from about 1500 onwards there is a marked increase of Mycenaean influence noticeable in Cretan art. It has been plausibly argued that from *c.* 1450 until the eclipse of Knossos half a century later (probably through a combination of earthquake, revolt and a well-timed raid from the mainland) Crete was in fact ruled by a Mycenaean dynasty. Perhaps the mercenary commander of the palace guard staged a *coup*, or even married into the priest-king's family. Cretan scribes would be thereupon forced to adapt their written syllabary for the expression of a new 'ruling-class language' – Mycenaean Greek. The result (so brilliantly deciphered by Michael Ventris) was the cumbersome script now famous as Linear B, incised on clay tablets, and baked hard in the final conflagration which destroyed its users (*c.* 1400).

What strikes us most forcibly about this 'Palace Civilization' (prior to its infiltration by mainland influences) is its sophisticated and affluent elegance. Never again until the days of Imperial Rome do we find such stylish comfort, such sensuous delight in natural phenomena, such unselfconscious zest for living. At Knossos the Queen had her own private bathroom, equipped with running water and the equivalent of a flush toilet. Flat Mediterranean-type roofs made it easy to build on additions in any direction, while the use of light-wells illuminated even the most labyrinthine structure. The intricate pottery designs, with their bird, fish and flower motifs, the figurines of ivory and faience (including the famous snake-goddesses), the silver plate, the fantastic gold jewellery (employing filigree and granulation techniques, the latter only recently rediscovered), the carved seal-rings with their charging bulls and bare-breasted priestesses – all these are imbued with a lightness, a delicacy, a fluid and sensuous hedonism that are uniquely Minoan. This delirious dance of colour and the senses, this fascination with plant and animal life, with sex and social intercourse and religious ritual, with the stylized dangers of boxing and bull-vaulting, reveals a life-style clear outside the mainstream of European history.

22 Faience 'house' plaques from Knossos (*c.* 1750 BC).

23 Right: open stone drains at Knossos.

24 Left: acrobat and drinking bull: impression from a Minoan onyx seal (1750–1570 BC).

25 Centre left: gold signet-ring from Isopata, near Knossos (c. 1500 BC) showing dancing women (sometimes identified as tree-goddesses).

26 Below left: Late Minoan clay bath-tub from Pachyammos near Gournia.

27 Below: faience snake-goddess from the Treasury of the Central Sanctuary, Knossos (c. 1500 BC).

31

28 Detail from the Blue Bird fresco (*c.* 1500 BC), a garden fresco from the so-called 'House of the Frescoes' on the 'Royal Road', north of the Palace at Knossos.

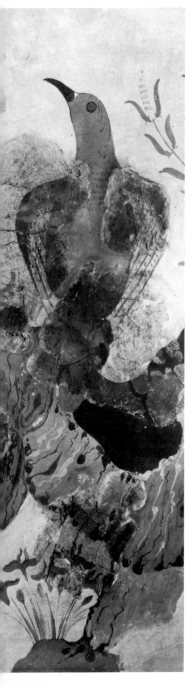

But it is the frescoes which have most caught people's imagination, and rightly so, since not only do they have great intrinsic value as art, but also offer tantalizing glimpses into the social life and religious preoccupations of Cretan civilization at its zenith. We can divide them into two main groups: scenes of palace life and scenes from nature. The latter show animals in their open-air surroundings: monkeys, flying fish, a deer jumping over rocks and flowers, a cat stalking a pheasant. In the Temple Fresco and the Blue Fresco court ladies sit and chatter to one another when they should, in all likelihood, have been attending to some spectacle or ceremony (*cf.* modern Italian or Greek churchgoers). The most famous fragment of the so-called 'Campstool Fresco', in which young people are sitting on stools and seemingly drinking each others' health, is a profile portrait, 'La Parisienne', which does indeed suggest nothing so much as a French lady of the nineties, complete with carmine lipstick, eyeshadow and a most elaborate kiss-curl coiffure. Nature and human figures coalesce in the famous Bull-Leaper Fresco (*c.* 1500). The trick of the leap (much debated) was for the torero to get between the bull's horns as it charged, and then to vault over its back, either hands first, feet first, or – as one seal suggests – by backward somersault.

29 Opposite right: woman's head, known popularly as 'La Parisienne', probably a fragment of the 'Campstool Fresco' found in the upper storey of the West Block, Knossos (*c.* 1500 BC). Modern opinion (and restorations) to the contrary, it would seem that in Crete only snake-goddesses and priestesses 'went topless', probably for ritual purposes. Otherwise, as here, some sort of dress or Tyrolean-type blouse seems to have been worn.

30 Bull-Leaper fresco, from the Palace of Knossos (shortly after 1500 BC). Bull-leaping was a daring feat practised by young Minoan men and girls. They literally grasped the bull by the horns and vaulted or somersaulted over him.

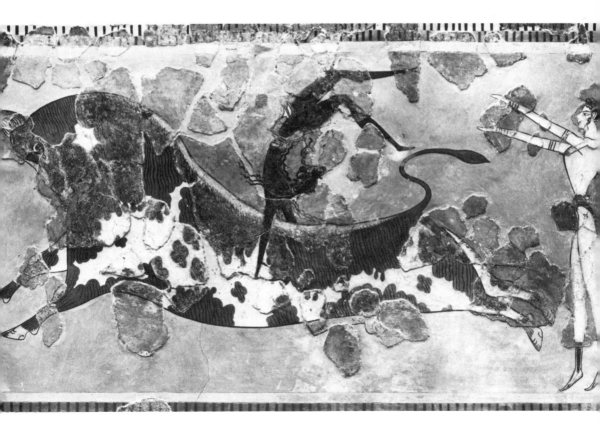

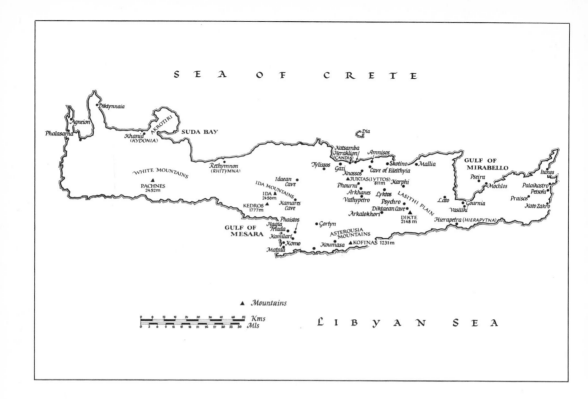

SEA OF CRETE

GULF OF MIRABELLO

WHITE MOUNTAINS
PACHNES 2452m

IDA MOUNTAINS
IDA 2456m

KEDROS 1777m

GULF OF MESARA

ASTEROUSIA MOUNTAINS
KOFINAS 1231m

DIKTE 2148 m

LASITHI PLAIN

▲ Mountains

Kms
Mls

LIBYAN SEA

31 Map of Crete. Crete's isolation in the Aegean is further reinforced by a rocky and forbidding southern coast, and the great mountain ranges which dominate the island, seamed with limestone caves, and offering an ideal fastness for brigands or guerrillas.

32 Opposite, top left: the sacred grotto of Eileithyia, goddess of childbirth, at Amnisos, on the north coast near Knossos. Excavation reveals that the cave was sacred to a chthonian fertility goddess as early as the Neolithic period.

33 Opposite, top right: caves had considerable religious significance in Minoan life. Here we have numbers of tiny bronze bulls, *ex-voto* offerings, from the cave of Diktaean Zeus on the Lassithi Plain in East Crete.

What we find on Crete, then, is a civilization fundamentally different from any which succeeded or (as far as we can tell) preceded it. Whereas the classical Greeks saw nature as an enemy, to be fought and bested, the Minoans went *with* nature, even if nature retorted by rumbling bull-like underground and knocking down their best palaces. They might best be described as high-class hedonists with a strong religious sense; and their religion, characteristically, seems to have been a gay open-air everyday faith, with holy spots on mountaintops and in groves or by springs and well-houses, with fertility goddesses and an Artemis-like Mistress of Beasts, and double axes, and a tradition, long remembered, which thought of the afterworld not in terms of gloomy Hades, but as a happy sunlit paradise, Elysium, ruled over by Cretan Rhadamanthus, the judge of the dead. Like all true hedonists, the Minoans lacked that nagging urge (so prevalent in later ages) to reorganize the world rationally for its own good. Nor do we find them manifesting a Protagorean urge to place Man – sculpturally or otherwise inflated – at the centre of the universe, let alone build grim protective fortifications (whether physical or spiritual) round his puny achievements. For that we must turn to the Mycenaeans, who, even at several removes, show themselves the Greeks' true ancestors in a way the Cretans never were.

34, 35 The double-axe (*lab-raunda*), like the so-called 'horns of consecration' (*cf.* pl. 18) is a recurrent religious symbol in Minoan art – as here, incised in the north wall of the Palace at Knossos (left) or fashioned elaborately in gold, a splendid specimen from Arkalochori, *c.* 1500 BC (above).

36 Below: typical steato-
pygous Cycladic figure from
Eleusis (*c.* 2000 BC). Such
figurines occur throughout the
Aegean and the Near East: the
mother-goddess cult they imply never completely died out
in antiquity.

37 The Asprochalikó cave, or
rock shelter, between Ioannina
and Arta in north-west Greece,
where there were recently
(1965) found the oldest known
habitation site in Greece, and
extensive stratified deposits of
the Middle and Upper Palaeolithic periods (*c.* 40,000 to
13,000 BC).

The Mycenaean Age

Inhabitation of the Balkan peninsula has now been traced back for at
least sixty to seventy thousand years: even this figure is both conservative and provisional. Recently (1960) the skull of a Neanderthaler
was found near Petralona in Chalcidice. Hunters of the Middle and
Late Palaeolithic Ages left scattered flints and other artefacts along the
banks of the River Peneus in Thessaly. Flint factories discovered on
islands such as Scyros and Zacynthos show that as early as 9000 BC
Aegean man was crossing the sea on rafts and trading in obsidian.
But the really important change (as with almost any known society)
came with the transition from Mesolithic to Neolithic, from a hunting
to a farming economy. Carbon-14 tests indicate that the earliest Neolithic settlers reached Greece during the seventh millennium. Their
first concern was for good pasturage: this drew them to the plains of
Thessaly or Boeotia, and the land round the Gulf of Argos. They did
not possess the plough, and their lack of farming expertise is hinted at
by the number of fertility idols they left behind: small, dumpy female
figurines carved from serpentine or greenstone, with huge buttocks

and coffee-bean eyes, typical of the ubiquitous Near East mother-goddess cult.

A concentric series of ring-wall defences at Dhimini in Thessaly, one of the latest-surviving (*c.* 2500 B C) among these Stone Age sites, shows that the transition from a Neolithic to a metal-working culture during the first half of the third millennium was not always peacefully accomplished. The site as a whole much resembles a sheepfold (literally as well as symbolically), and one sure precipitant of centralized government is collective defence against some external threat. It has even been suggested that the central keep of Dhimini implies a rudimentary *polis* régime, and that 'the first important fact in the political history of Europe is visible here' (Lévêque, p. 11). In any case, the occupation of the Greek mainland by these shadowy invaders from Anatolia was a slow (if ultimately beneficial) process. In addition to bronze, and the metal-working techniques which went with it, they also brought the swing-plough. Stabilization of agriculture led to permanent settlements under local barons, each ruling an area of up to ten miles' radius round a walled hilltop site. Trade, especially by sea, began to flourish, with a consequent differentiation of social status through wealth (*e.g.* stone houses as against mud-brick). Commercialization brought specialist craftsmen, the beginnings of agricultural urbanism (political as well as economic) and the first use of symbols – seals, pot-marks, tallies, trade-signs – to convey a message. Early Helladic I (*c.* 2800–2600 B C), a period of social and technological transition, was succeeded by Early Helladic II (*c.* 2600–2100 B C), which capitalized and developed these new advances, and has been described by an eminent archaeologist as 'one of the most potentially civilized societies Greece ever had' (Vermeule, p. 31). For the modern student its most remarkable monument is the elegant House of the Tiles at Lerna, a lush site on the Gulf of Argos where Heracles, according to tradition, overcame the many-headed Hydra.

But Lerna, like many other EH II sites in Greece, fell victim, about 2100 B C, to a wave of alien invaders, the so-called 'Patterned Ware' people: marauding barbarians who burnt and destroyed this delightful site (though superstitious dread made them wall off the ruined House of the Tiles like some infectious plague-spot). These newcomers formed the first spearhead of a vast collective migrant movement, the shock-waves of which were felt throughout Europe. It originated somewhere in the great plateaux of central Asia, sweeping west and south from Russia across the Danube, and penetrating the Balkans from the north. (The Hittite occupation of Asia Minor can be correlated with this general upheaval, as can the establishment of Troy VI, with its great batter walls, its horses and textiles and wheel-made pottery.) A second and larger incursion, *c.* 1950–1900, was

38, 39 Clay sealings from the House of the Tiles, Lerna (*c.* 2200 BC). Seals in the Bronze Age were used to close storage jars, chests, doors, boxes and baskets; they could be worn round the neck like amulets, or used as die-stamps for decorative patterns.

40 View from the north-west of the House of the Tiles, Lerna, the most remarkable surviving example of Early Helladic II culture (*c.* 2200 BC), but destroyed very soon after it was built. Its modern name refers to the roof-tiles of terracotta and bluish schist found *in situ* by archaeologists. Corridors, red stucco wall-panels, windows, wooden door-jambs – all testify to a high degree of taste and civilization.

accompanied by widespread devastation of fortified towns (though many smaller centres escaped). At site after site, especially in the Argolid, we find tell-tale ash-layers, blackened pottery, evidence of wanton destruction.

We do not know what these people called themselves. Their pottery, oddly soapy to the touch, and made in imitation of a metal original, with sharp flanges sliced against a turning wheel, was first found by Schliemann at Orchomenus: mindful as ever of local myth, he labelled both it and them 'Minyan', a title which (like 'Minoan') may be unhistorical but at least has the merit of convenience. The language they spoke was a branch of the Indo-European group, and they are thus entitled to be regarded as the first true Greeks. With their arrival, those steatopygous female fertility images so popular in the Neolithic period largely vanish, to be replaced by hilltop or acropolis sanctuaries. The invaders seem to have brought with them not only a typically Indo-European male sky-god cult, but also a feudal, palace-based society somewhat akin to that of Homer's Olympians (who may be an echo, at many removes, of these conquering warrior-aristocrats). However, the indigenous inhabitants had a good deal to offer which the 'Minyans' lacked: techniques for cultivating the vine and olive, and above all maritime expertise. One disadvantage under which these newcomers laboured was that of total ignorance of sea-faring in a country where the sea was essential to civilized life. Once they took to ships – taught, perhaps, by the Cycladic islanders – they became great Mediterranean traders; but the process of acclimatization was, inevitably, a slow one. Social growth and development, once this mixed population had settled down together, there must have been: overseas development will have brought some mainlanders at least into contact with the brilliant culture of Crete, and perhaps that of Egypt as well. Yet there is nothing in this Middle Helladic world which foreshadows the sudden amazing explosion of wealth and power symbolized, for us, by the Shaft Graves at Mycenae.

Of these two grave circles, one (Circle A) was found by Schliemann in 1876, the other (Circle B) by Greek archaeologists as recently as 1951. Circle B is the earlier by at least a century, dating from *c.* 1600 B C. Excavation has revealed no trace of any settlement relating to either of them: the graves themselves, and their contents, stood alone as a memorial to posterity (Circle A was brought inside the Mycenaean citadel during a major rebuilding scheme after 1300, and marked off with a circle of stones as sacred ground, rather like the House of the Tiles at Lerna). The contents strike a utilitarian rather than a religious note: no cult-images, but fabulous loot galore –

41 View of the Shaft Grave Circle and granary, Mycenae. This is Circle A, excavated by Schliemann: Circle B is outside the walls, near the so-called 'Tomb of Clytaemnestra'. The granary was erected inside the citadel to supply its defenders with stored grain when Mycenae was under siege.

42 Top: rock-crystal dish in the form of a duck, from Grave Circle B, Mycenae (*c.* 1600 BC).

43 Above: gold burial mask (called by Schliemann the 'Mask of Agamemnon') from Shaft Grave V, Grave Circle A, Mycenae.

44 Above right: Mycenaean contacts with the Orient are shown by this ivory pyxis lid, with its winged griffin, carved from a cross-section of a tusk: from a tomb at Athens (*c.* 1400 BC).

45 Opposite, top: seal-stone of amethyst, showing bearded head in profile, from Grave Circle B (Graves Gamma and Omicron), Mycenae, *c.* 1600 BC.

46 Opposite, below: heads of Mycenaean men, in gold and black niello, probably from a cup-decoration: from the Palace at Englianos, near Pylos.

bronze swords, inlaid daggers, rings, engraved gems, a crystal duck bowl and endless gold ornaments. 'Rich in gold' is Homer's epithet for Mycenae, and here indeed the gold was: embossed cups, bracelets, necklaces, and the inscrutable moustachioed death-masks which led Schliemann – understandably, though he was in fact over two centuries out in his dating – to cable the King of Prussia: 'I have looked upon the face of Agamemnon.'

Who were the owners of this royal treasure? Where did they, and it, come from? What led them to Mycenae? Their funeral stelae reveal them as warriors and hunters: one remarkable miniature portrait, carved on a seal-stone, has certain characteristic features – high cheekbones, prominent eyeridges, aggressive beard, aquiline nose – of the eternal European aristocrat. With their long swords, their chariots and horses, and their accumulated plunder (presumably acquired through successful military ventures) they form a striking contrast to the beardless, unwarlike exquisites of Crete. One attractive and convincing theory identifies them with the mythical Danaans, who, though *barbaroi* from Egypt, ended as kings in the Peloponnese (F. H. Stubbings, CAH II², 3rd ed., fasc. 14, pp. 11 ff). Danaus himself, the founder, thus becomes a Hyksos refugee (*c.* 1600–1570) who took over Mycenae and established a 'Shaft Grave dynasty' which lasted for several generations, until the death of Eurystheus and his replacement by the Achaean 'sons of Pelops' – a take-over perhaps confirmed by the change (*c.* 1500 at Mycenae) from shaft-graves to *tholos* (beehive) tombs for royal burials. (The latter, significantly, antedate any secular large-scale domestic architecture: a *tholos*, clearly, was regarded as a more desirable status symbol than a palace.) The two centuries between 1500 and 1300 mark the apogee of Mycenaean civilization, with overseas trade steadily developing at the expense of Crete, and from about 1450 until 1400 (*see* p. 30) a Mycenaean dynasty actually established in Knossos.

We can picture Mycenaean Greece split up into a number of small but heavily administered districts (to regard Mycenae itself as in any sense a 'capital' is misleading), with a scribal caste at the service of warrior leaders, a vigorous commercial economy, a high level of craftsmanship (mostly imported) and a tradition of internecine warfare and bickering, probably exacerbated by dynastic inter-marriages and a rising population, with too many younger sons chasing too few fiefs, and tending to take up mercenary service, in Crete or Egypt or elsewhere, as a result. (Some emigrated to northern Greece: their descendants subsequently returned at the head of the Dorian invaders.) From about 1300 onwards, however, despite its elaborate and all-pervasive bureaucracy, the Mycenaean world began, slowly but unmistakably, to lose ground. Its commercial empire first shrank, and then disintegrated. Pottery exports dwindled away, especially in the eastern Mediterranean. Sea-raiders and pirates preyed on the hitherto inviolate shipping-lanes: international trade seems to have been almost totally disrupted. It was now, too, that great Cyclopean walls rose around important centres such as Thebes, Gla, Tiryns, Iolcos or Mycenae itself, turning them into fortress-strongholds. What prompted such elaborate defensive architecture? Obviously, fear of imminent attack, either by some external enemy, or else from rival baronies (a conflict due, it would seem, to over-population, and perhaps reflected in the myth of the *Seven against Thebes*, with Polyneices bringing Argive supporters to help him oust the Theban dynasty of Eteocles).

During the mid thirteenth century B C – perhaps while many Achaean barons, together with their best troops, were campaigning in Asia Minor – several Peloponnesian sites, Mycenae included, suffered severe damage. That this was the work of invaders from the north is compatible with myth, and made plain by the great Cyclopean wall across the Isthmus of Corinth, built shortly afterwards (*c.* 1220–1200) in a last desperate effort to ward off further attacks. The attempt ultimately failed: one circumstantial myth records an invasion across the Corinthian Gulf, at its narrowest point. Within a century every major Mycenaean stronghold had fallen, never to be recovered. It is against this ominous *Götterdämmerung* background that we must view the events immortalized by Homer in his *Iliad*: a tenuous epic thread reaching back beyond the Dark Ages to Agamemnon's doomed citadel and the (equally real, equally romanticized) fallen splendours of Troy.

47 Below: detail from the 'Warrior Vase', a krater from the Citadel, Mycenae (*c.* 1200 BC). Despite such military emphasis, Mycenae was to fall within a century.

48 Far left: ivory figure of a Mycenaean warrior with helmet, spear and figure-of-eight shield: from Delos (1400–1200 BC). The contrast between such figures and the gay Cretans of the frescoes is most striking.

49 Left: upper part of a silver funnel-shaped rhyton (Citadel of Mycenae, Grave IV). The relief, partly preserved, shows Mycenaean troops disembarking for an assault on a town, under fire from enemy archers and slingers.

50 Below: aerial view of the Mycenaean fortress of Tiryns: its vast Cyclopean enceinte has astonished visitors from Pausanias' day to our own.

From Troy to Homer

The mid thirteenth century, with its disruptive sea-raiders, its continual vague threat of vast migrant hordes emerging from the Eurasian steppes, its baronial factionalism and over-population (the cause of the Trojan War, one epic fragment claims), its landless men with good pedigrees and ready swords seeking an inheritance, preferably not by trade – here, surely, is the ideal breeding-ground for a 'heroic age', which in economic terms means stealing other men's capital instead of producing your own, and evolving an aristocratic warrior-code to justify the process. In a period when the old Mediterranean-wide trading facilities had become severely curtailed, and too many noblemen's younger sons were chasing too little in the way of rich pickings, Troy formed the obvious and natural target for a Viking-style raid. It had been rich and prosperous for centuries. Though badly shaken by the great earthquake which (*c.* 1300) ended Troy VI, it was still – with its textile and metal-working industries, its horsebreeding, and the accumulated treasure these activities brought in – a prize well worth the taking.

Perhaps about 1250–1240, and thus little more than a generation before the Greek mainland sites (*e.g.* Pylos) themselves began to fall, Troy VIIa was sacked and burnt, after a prolonged siege: Professor Carl W. Blegen's excavations strikingly confirm the Homeric

51 House in Troy VIIA (*c.* 1250 BC). Such houses were crowded, like squatters' shacks, inside the walls: large storage jars sunk almost flush with the ground hint at a long siege. They perished in what Blegen calls 'a devastating conflagration' – almost certainly during the Achaean sack recorded by Homer.

tradition. Myth and archaeology here corroborate one another: both show a brief Trojan reoccupation of the city (VIIb 1), both confirm a peaceful infiltration from central Europe, about 1200, by the so-called 'Knobbed Ware' people (VIIb 2), and both indicate a final destruction of the settlement *c.* 1100, at the outset of that general population shift into the Balkans which today we know (perhaps misleadingly) as the 'Coming of the Dorians'. Despite much embroidery and numerous anachronistic accretions from his own background (that of eighth-century Ionia) Homer, it is safe to say, rests on a firm central stratum of historical fact. It is even possible (as many 'Peloponnesian' myths suggest) that the prolonged absence of these Achaean warlords at Troy materially contributed to the collapse of Mycenaean power in Greece itself. By 1100, at all events, all the main centres had fallen to attacks from the north. For a while an impoverished version of Mycenaean culture – aptly known as 'sub-Mycenaean' – struggled on; then that too faded from sight.

As at the turn of the second millennium, there would seem to have been two separate waves of invasion: the first about 1200–1190, the second rather less than a century later. Both, again, can be related to a general mass migration from central Asia, a vast anonymous horde with horned helmets and ox-drawn covered wagons (both suggestive of northern pastoral origins), which made its way, locust-like, across the Hellespont, through the Hittite Empire, by way of Cilicia and the Phoenician coast to the very gates of Egypt, where Rameses III held and defeated them in two great battles. The curious fact is that after this defeat we simply have no idea what became of them. They vanish amid the wreckage of the civilizations they had destroyed, fading into the darkness of the next four centuries – for which they had been as responsible as anyone. This period (*c.* 1150–750) was more of a blank to Greeks of the historical period than it is to us. Historians like Herodotus and Thucydides vaguely knew that there had been a time when the Greeks spoke a different language. They had a body of myth about Troy and Thebes and the so-called 'Return of the sons of Heracles' (that is, the infiltration, from about 1100, of Dorian tribes-men, led, according to tradition, by exiled Mycenaean barons from the north). But they knew nothing whatsoever about the great bureaucratic palace cultures, and hence underestimated the degree of cultural fragmentation which had taken place. The result was a drastic oversimplifying of the past, an odd foreshortening process, historical syncretism.

The Dorians, however elusive they may be archaeologically (an irritating trait, characteristic of all nomads) were certainly real enough. Their arrival from north-west Greece is marked by changes in dialect and burial customs, the increased use of iron (what Gordon Childe called the 'democratic metal') instead of bronze, the introduction of large fibulae, or pins, to fasten a presumably blanket-like garment, and the first appearance of what we term Protogeometric pottery, with its neat compass-drawn circles, broad bands and symmetrical patterns. Athens, according to tradition, never fell. Once again myth is triumphantly vindicated by archaeology, which reveals clear cultural continuity in the pottery sequences, and, on the Acropolis itself, an inner staircase leading down to an inner spring – like that of Mycenae – which was clearly used during siege. It is unconquered Athens we have to thank for what survives of the Mycenaean legends, though Mycenaean customs and culture soon vanished with the great palaces and the scribal bureaucracies dependent on them. Otherwise only remote areas like Arcadia escaped the Dorians; and where the latter found good arable land or pasturage – Sparta, Thessaly, to some extent Messenia – they remained a separate body, conquerors ruling over indigenous serfs.

One last important change took place to create the Aegean ethnic and cultural pattern we know from historical times. Over a period of nearly two centuries, beginning soon after 1100, we find a series of eastward migrations taking place, from mainland Greece to the coast of Asia Minor. In the first instance this movement was clearly a Mycenaean refugee phenomenon, a diaspora. It can be divided into three separate sections, best visualized as horizontal bands running

52 The grave of a young girl, Protogeometric period (*c.* 1000 BC), from the Agora, Athens.

from west to east. The mythic tradition confirms all main details known from dialect distributions and archaeology, but, again, telescopes a long process into one well-organized expedition in each case. In the north we find refugees from Thessaly and Boeotia moving across to Lesbos, the Troad and the adjacent mainland, and speaking the dialect known as 'Aeolic'. The rich central strip of Ionia, with its alluvial plains and great river-valleys, was colonized – after a bitter struggle – immediately after the Dorians overran mainland Greece: Athens traditionally supplied the leaders for this expedition. Later, perhaps about 900, the Dorians themselves spread out eastward from the Peloponnese, island-hopping by way of Melos, Thera and Rhodes to south-west Caria. The Greek world as we know it from classical times was now complete, except for the great colonization movement two centuries later (*see* p. 49), which added Sicily and southern Italy – among other areas – to the Hellenic orbit. These cities kept up the traditions, dialects and cults of their various ethnic groups (Aeolic, Ionic or Doric). At the same time they controlled both the maritime and overland trade-routes of Anatolia, which provided them with a remarkably cosmopolitan (not to say polyglot) background.

By 800 there was, broadly speaking, unity of language and, to some extent, of culture throughout the Aegean world. The rediscovery of writing, this time with a viable alphabet rather than a restricted syllabary, was in the offing. Pottery forms, if not identical, were at

53 Detail from a large Geometric amphora or 'Dipylon vase' (so named from the area in Athens where the type was excavated), used as a grave-marker (*c.* 750 BC). The scene shows men (standing) and women (kneeling) in mourning before a high bier on which the corpse lies in state (prothesis).

least cognate everywhere: trade and communications had, clearly, been restored. Human figures do not reappear on vases (beside the horses and deer) till *c.* 750 – about the time, perhaps, that Homer was composing the *Iliad* and *Odyssey* – and even then they are dwarfed by band after band of geometrical design, the eternally recurrent meander or 'Greek key'. Indeed, they are made as nearly geometric as possible themselves. They appear mainly on the huge funeral vases, some over six feet high, placed as markers over graves in the Cerameicus cemetery of Athens, and pierced at the bottom to let libations flow down to the dead man. And here we may glimpse an odd parallel in the creative atmosphere of the age. There is no gradual growth about these vases; they go at one stroke from normal to giant proportions. Similarly, it has been suggested, the oral lays of Mycenaean epic were welded into a greater whole by one bard who dared (as did a few potters) to conceive on an unprecedentedly vast scale. Something about the mid-eighth-century atmosphere, a sense of exhilaration, of widening emotional horizons, must have encouraged this crucial leap. Here, surely, was the moment at which the true germination of the Greek creative genius took place – with Homer as its first (and never-to-be-surpassed) exponent.

The Greek world which Homer knew (as opposed to the syncretic Mycenaean age he drew in his poems) was desperately poor, a series of small isolated communities, each clustering round a hilltop 'big house' run on feudal lines by some local warrior-baron. Kingship, the rule of the *wanax*, was largely obsolete. The Dark Age practice of relying on a local chieftain for protection was encouraged by the canton-like geography of Greece, and proved oddly persistent: it foreshadows the city-state in embryo. Something of this contemporary world is reflected by Homer: impoverished princes who dig their own gardens while their womenfolk do their own laundry and weaving.

Yet the dominant pattern in Homeric epic is retrospective, nostalgic, fiercely reactionary. It looks back five centuries to a kingly age of heroes, to golden Mycenae, the social and political institutions of which (except for an occasional embedded survival, *e.g.* the court of Nestor at Messenian Pylos) it has completely forgotten. The *Iliad* reveals an absolute split between nobles and populace. It hints at a tradition based on the memories of men whose ancestors (many of them Mycenaean refugees) had sailed eastward from the chaos of Dorian Greece to build a new world in Ionia and preserve, if they could, some recollection of the old. The fact that Homer's brilliant (if largely fanciful) enshrinement of a long-dead civilization not only survived, but became a combined Bible, moral code and source of practical wisdom for all Greeks of the classical age, remains one of the greatest paradoxes in European history.

2

The crystallization of the city-state (750–600 BC)

Expansion and colonization

After the slow recovery of the Dark Ages there came a sudden spurt, an accelerated cultural, political and intellectual efflorescence, associated with what is known (rather misleadingly) as the 'Archaic Period' (c. 750–480 BC). This title suggests static conservatism: nothing could be further from the truth, and Professor Chester G. Starr's 'Age of Revolution' is a far more accurate description. This period can be divided, for convenience, into two halves, at a point between 650 and 600 BC. Before then we have the reintroduction of writing, itself probably stimulated by a resurgence in seagoing trade about the middle of the eighth century. Settled conditions, and a consequent population increase, also encouraged a vast colonizing movement from mainland Greece and Ionia, to points as far afield as the Black Sea, Sicily, southern Italy (so popular that it became known as 'Great Greece', the Roman Magna Graecia), and the Franco-Spanish coast. Trade with the Near East brought not only Orienta-lizing influences, but also a flood of new intellectual ideas and eastern myths.

Kingship had almost everywhere given way to government through a hereditary aristocracy, based on landownership reinforced by profit-able commerce. During the period 750–600, however, capital (with the expansion of trade on a Mediterranean-wide basis) became more mobile; non-aristocrats at once saw a chance to improve their position, politically as well as socially (often allying themselves with politically frustrated noble families, to the ultimate benefit of both parties); predictable tensions began to build up between the ruling classes and those traditionally subordinate to them. An increased emphasis on divine ancestry and genealogical sanctions hints that the

54 Obverse of an early Athen-ian tetradrachm showing the helmeted head of Athena. First struck by the Peisistra-tids, these 'Attic owls' both symbolized Attic unity and, later, came to embody Athens' commercial-imperial supremacy.

55 Attic Geometric wine-pourer: note the neat, schematic decoration, including the famous meander, or 'Greek key' pattern.

hereditary principle was now under pressure from men whose power derived from property rather than breeding – a supposition confirmed by subsequent political reforms, all heavily loaded in favour of capital. By about 570 B C many Greek states – Attica in particular – found themselves confronted with a political crisis which only the most drastic measures, leading in the end to complete, if piecemeal, political revolution, could adequately solve.

In this revolutionary process (which was at least as much intellectual and artistic as political) the spread of literacy played a crucial role. It paved the way for that extraordinary breakthrough of reason, the so-called 'Greek miracle', in sixth-century Ionia (see pp. 96 ff.). A more immediate result – and equally momentous in political terms – was the establishment of legal codes for the various city-states. This struck a mortal blow at the arbitrary rule of priest or baron by making available a body of acceptable and accepted public precedent to which all free men could appeal. It was the beginning of civic government, of rational law and order.

Here we hit on one of the two main leitmotivs detectable in the Archaic Age. If the first, and more obvious, of these is discovery – exploration in both the literal and the figurative sense – the more fundamental remains the process of settlement, of codification. The first expanded men's vision, gave them greater flexibility of judgment by tearing them free from their old narrow confines, and thrusting

them into a new world where they had to improvise their own rules: no accident that the law-givers – *e.g.* Solon of Athens, Charondas of Catania – were also reformers. But equally, a counterbalance to this freewheeling creative instinct, we find a strong impulse to set the world in order, to rationalize it, and (the great intellectual advance) to make generalizations about its processes.

The significant element in this trend is its purely secular nature. Terror of chaos (after the Dark Ages, which had had chaos in plenty) may have been one motive behind all the tidy pattern-making: few things, after all, are so mathematically rational as a Late Geometric vase. It may also explain why the Greeks persisted so obstinately in maintaining their minuscule political units, even in areas (such as Sicily and southern Italy) where they were patently inappropriate. Against this civic parochialism – to which there were exceptions – we must set the growing concept of 'Hellenism' as such, a community of language, speech and cult, symbolized by the great international athletic festivals, held (under religious auspices) at Olympia, Delphi and elsewhere. During this period the stone temple came into fashion, and developed in the most remarkable way. Sculptors began to work on a large scale in stone and bronze, advancing from figurines to representation of the ideal nude male (*kouros*). The Olympian gods, and their cults, were everywhere in evidence, though more as a focal point for civic pride than as an expression of true religious feeling.

56 Opposite, below: the 'Municipal Laws' of Gortyn, Crete (formulated 500 BC, but illustrating a trend of codification almost two centuries older). The text is written *boustrophedon*, 'as the plough-ox turns', each alternate line being – for us – mirror-image, running from right to left.

57, 58, 59 Below, left to right: archaic ivory *kore* figurine from the Dipylon, Athens (*c.* 730 BC); wooden statuette of Hera from Samos (*c.* 660 BC); bronze *kouros*-type statuette of Apollo from Piraeus (700–600 BC).

60 Statue of the youth Kroisos (*c.* 525 BC). This rather lumpish *kouros* well illustrates the problems confronting early sculptors who chose to work on a life-size scale.

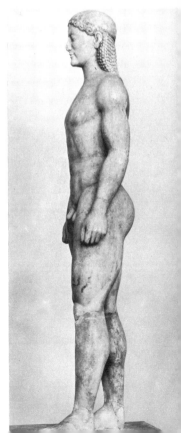

61, 62 One aspect of colonization was conflict at sea between
Greek and Etruscan vessels.
In these details from a (probably West Greek) krater signed
by Aristonothos (*c.* 660 BC),
two ships are shown bows on.
The left-hand one is of the
Greek type, with ram; the
right-hand one may be an
Etruscan merchantman pre-
paring to resist attack.

Hominocentrism is the keynote here. It was, precisely, the ability
to form abstract laws which opened the way both to scientific speculation and to *polis* government: the two things went hand in hand. It is
the firm attachment of moral values (at least among the educated) to
secular ethical principles which gives the Greek gods of the classical
period the air of having stepped out of some well-read freethinker's
library. The bland anthropomorphism of Homer's gods jars on
modern sensibilities, but cannot be ignored. These Olympians are
simply outsize human beings, with larger-than-life human weaknesses,
living in glorified Mycenaean *megara* and enjoying their immortality,
their unlimited power, like so many irresponsible children – or tribal
elders. To get the horripilating numinous impact of divinity we have
to go to deities outside the inner Olympian circle, like Demeter or
Dionysus, demotic gods of grain and wine, bound up with violent
human emotions and worshipped seasonally by the common people.
A clear class distinction can be observed here. Olympianism much
resembled an established church, a heavenly projection of the
aristocratic ideal. This, too, was where the secular emphasis fell. Most
gentlemen may have been pious conservatives; but the spearhead of
intellectual innovation was always closely bound up with the ruling
classes. This spirit of what Herodotus afterwards called *historie*,
rational inquiry, permeates the entire period: it is what gives Greek
culture its characteristic flavour.

The arbitrary amoralism of the old patriarchal deities proved a horrible embarrassment to sages who were discovering the joys of rational ethics and civic-mindedness, and had little time for the traditions of clan or kinship group. The centrifugalism of eighth-century colonization did more than promote trade and undermine aristocratic power: it made subtle inroads on traditionalism in every form. From Spain and Sicily, from Egypt and the Black Sea, new ideas, beliefs and customs were fed back along the trade-routes, travelling in the grain-ships like invisible plague rats. Yet the Greeks showed a singular ability to master and adapt even their most exotic imports. The so-called 'Orientalizing' art of the seventh century BC is a good case in point. We have a sudden influx of wild beasts and imaginary monsters: gorgons, sphinxes, griffins, sirens, cruel-beaked powerful creatures of nightmare, savaging cattle or warriors with equal ferocity. Perhaps on their first introduction such creatures answered a sense of formless terror and chaos in the Greek mind; but by 600 BC all their horror has gone, formalized into endurable concepts, the crudeness transmuted by art. Medusa becomes a comic apotropaic, griffin-heads are much in demand as lugs for cauldrons. (One bronze plaque from Olympia even shows a mother griffin guarding her young: domestication of the fearful could hardly go further.) Just so, in the fifth century, Aeschylus took the Furies and archaic Zeus and reconciled them with the ethical world of the *polis*.

63 Bronze cauldron-handle in the form of a (moderately fierce) griffin, from Olympia, late eighth century BC.

64 Opposite, far left; ivory statuette of a high priest, a Greek work showing Oriental influence (Ephesus, eighth–seventh century BC).

65, 66, 67, 68, 69 The domestication of mythical and other beasts was typical of 'Orientalizing' art. Far left: griffin with young, drawing after the cut-out bronze plaque seen left, incised in detail (probably the blazon of a wooden shield), from Olympia, late seventh century BC. Below, left: a throne with ivory inlay, sphinx and lotus motifs, showing Orientalizing influence; centre, an ivory bedframe from a tomb; right, an ivory plaque carved with a winged sphinx, all from Cyprus (seventh century BC).

70 The blinding of Polyphemus: detail from the neck of a Protoattic funerary vase (Eleusis, *c.* 650 BC).

71 Above right: hoplite engagement (note the piper in rear); detail from the Chigi Vase, a Protocorinthian olpe from Veii (*c.* 650 BC). The anonymous Corinthian artist contrived to convey a remarkable sense of realism and perspective in miniature.

72, 73 Opposite, above: marble *kouros* from Sunium (*c.* 600 BC). The static Egyptian pose (as in the statue of Ranofer, a priest of Ptah at Memphis, below) is slowly changing to a more dynamic concept of the human form.

Till the mid seventh century human figures are still rare, but then scenes from epic and myth begin to appear (*e.g.* Odysseus blinding Polyphemus). There are also processions of heavyarmed soldiers, reflecting a major change in society at large (*see* pp. 62–3). It is no accident that one of the most popular figures with vasepainters during this period should be Heracles – the embodiment of muscular selfassertion, a primitive Superman fighting the forces of nature on mankind's behalf. *Homo faber* (if not *sapiens*) is moving steadily towards the centre of the stage. The transition had its difficulties: in particular, some external stimulus was needed, both in sculpture and in architecture, to achieve that *monumental* quality which typifies later Greek art. Rediscovered Egypt, with its gigantic temples and cultfigures, provided both. The astonishing thing is the way Greek artists transmuted what they found – adapting the pillared colonnade to a *megaron*style temple, imbuing stiffly stereotyped Egyptian statues with true dynamic plasticity.

The Delphic aphorisms – 'Know yourself' and 'Nothing too much' – might serve as epigraphs to the new age now dawning, in which men were ready, greatly daring, *hubris* warring against their consciousness of human frailty, to systematize the whole framework of creation. From now on the striving after order, causation and unity progressively extends to every facet of human existence. And undoubtedly one major factor in securing this release from the tyranny of traditional conformism had been the diaspora of Greeks throughout the Mediterranean, the throwing back of pioneers on their own judgments and resources. Self-reliance and originality: these are the qualities we associate with Odysseus rather than Achilles. They explain the popularity of the *Odyssey* in seventh-century Greek art, and they point forward towards that second stage in the Greek revolution which accompanied colonial expansion: the political and intellectual evolution of the city-state.

The ghost of Thersites

In the second book of the *Iliad* we meet, briefly, one of the most socially significant figures in Greek literature. Thersites – lame, bandy-legged, cowardly, ugly, garrulous and insubordinate – forms a classic antithesis to the *kalos k'agathos*, the gentleman of breeding who (for long after Homer) dominated city-state politics. Here is the eternal subverter of privileged law and order, the man from the masses who gets up and shouts the odds at his betters, the specialist in embarrassing home-truths. When we meet him (shortly after a demoralized rush to the ships by Agamemnon's war-weary veterans) he is the one man among the Achaeans talking unheroic common sense. Authority, in the person of Odysseus, has only one way of dealing with such a man: by brute force. Thersites, in fact, emerges as the first really vicious class caricature in European history, a combined scapegoat and bogey created by anxious clan-rulers who saw their own position, however vaguely, threatened from below. His very existence proves that some kind of protest was in the air, and had become vocal to a point where those in authority could not but be uneasily aware of it.

Between 750 and 600, in fact, the aristocratic principle of government came under increasingly heavy pressure. Class structure and economic pattern remained roughly the same, though the proportion of trade to agriculture had risen significantly by the end of the seventh century. The aristocracy still formed the most powerful, close-knit and independent sector of Greek society, with a life-style which, though leisurely, remained alert to new trends, and an inherited lion's share of the country's capital, mostly in land. Hitherto this had left them with all the profits and luxuries going. But colonization and the commercial growth which accompanied it had led to increased mobility of wealth. If fortunes could be acquired without pedigrees (in itself a revolutionary enough concept), why not political power? The success story of a non-titled usurper such as Gyges of Lydia (c. 685–?652 B C), who not only stole Candaules' wife and kingdom, but afterwards bribed an endorsement out of the Delphic Oracle, made it clear to talented, ambitious men outside the charmed inner circle that

inherited rule was not laid down in heaven, and that capital could, at a pinch, make a highly effective substitute for breeding. The whole idea of a *polis* society, of civic as opposed to clan justice, of elective (and, finally, collective) government was worked out, step by step, against this background.

To begin with, the aristocrats themselves were the chief traders, and soon developed a taste for imported luxuries – thus, all unawares, undermining their previously unassailable position. Little by little, trade and industry became genuine rivals to the landowner living off his estates. To pay for consumer goods, the latter would often sell off part of his property (*i.e.* convert frozen to liquid assets without fresh reinvestment, except in trading ventures, which through ship-wreck or piracy often came badly unstuck), and thus, on a long-term view, weaken his own economic position. This release of liquid capital, symbolized by the introduction to Greece (*c.* 600 B C) of coinage, a Lydian invention, inevitably heralded new political (though not social) standards. A proverb, 'Money makes the man', arose, which became the bitter slogan of *déclassé* reactionaries like Theognis (*see* p. 102). Since wealth, as opposed to blue blood, can in theory be acquired by anyone, the result was a step – unintentional, like most such developments – towards democracy.

Thersites, then, was an uncomfortable ghost, a presage of middle-class egalitarianism to come. His acerbic spirit lingered for quite a while, in poets like Hesiod and Archilochus; but finally it faded out again, because the civic revolution was by then an accomplished fact, flattering all free citizens with the illusion of power offered by an

74 Early Lydian electrum coin, from the reign of Croesus (561–?546 BC), showing the foreparts of lion and bull.

75, 76 Symbols of a two-class society: the chariot-borne war-rior and the patient plough-man. Right: Boeotian statuette in terracotta showing warrior with charioteer (seventh cen-tury BC); far right: bronze model ploughman with ox-team, possibly a votive offering (the right-hand ox is reversed; sixth century BC).

Assembly vote, while leaving the social fabric virtually intact. All Greek reformers, as we shall see, were reactionaries at heart (and not necessarily the worse for being so), who made an even nicer distinction than we do between social and political privileges. Thersites, in the last resort, could always – when force or bribery failed – be neutralized by grudging, piecemeal reform from within. But there was a short period, between the decline of the Homeric-style *basileus* ('baron' rather than 'king') and the full emergence of the *polis*, during which the individual voice could and did make itself heard, to memorable effect.

A classic case in point is Hesiod, the farmer-poet from Ascra, *fl.* *c.* 700 B C. This nagging, exhortatory character, well described as a fore-runner of the Presocratics, had an itch to sort out not only the world but the gods too: perhaps he saw both as an indistinguishable con-tinuum. The very fact that a mere lay poet took upon himself the priestly task of systematizing divine myth is a significant pointer to the temper of the age. Hesiod classified phenomena according to the only pattern he knew, that of the family tree (*genos*). He saw the world as a muddled, confusing, chaotic place (which in eighth-century Boeotia it must indeed have been) where the only hope lay in working out man's right relations with the gods, his fellow men, his natural environment, the weather, the sea around him, and all the rest of the messy, sprawling, half-known, barely controllable natural scene.

Hesiod is the spokesman of this transitional age in more ways than one. With him, Homeric morality, Homeric ideals are swept away under the pressure of brute necessity. The individual suddenly rises

out of the collective, thrusting, acquisitive, desperate. Though Hesiod betrays nostalgia for the good old days, he knows, from bitter personal experience, that it is the world he lives in with which men must come to terms. That curious work, the *Contest between Homer and Hesiod*, may be fictional in the strict sense, but it embodies much symbolic truth. The prize is awarded to Hesiod, on the grounds that he stands for peace and husbandry rather than for war and slaughter – a complete reversal of the heroic ideal. Here we see the new civic morality emerging in embryo; those who cannot enforce their wishes by *force majeure* or upper-class sanction must appeal to general principles because they have nothing else.

By Hesiod's day, the first hints of social discontent which Thersites symbolized have crystallized into a surly, articulate diatribe against corrupt and irresponsible *basileis*, now no more than local squires. Yet the *Works and Days* does not offer a programme of economic or political reform. Instead, Hesiod attacks the problem from a moral angle – though his promotion of hard work as the panacea for all ills is an uncharacteristic solution for a Greek: the 'gospel of labour' has never been popular in Mediterranean countries. His morality, like his theology, is that of the underprivileged, based on practical peasant self-interest; and his emphasis on the omnipotence of Zeus (echoes here of the Old Testament Jehovah) suggests a subject-race fantasizing divine vengeance in the hereafter against those who cannot be annihilated by main force here and now.

Though Hesiod sometimes appears to be preaching grim might-is-right pessimism (*e.g.* in his fable of the Hawk and the Nightingale, *Works and Days* 202 ff.), he also suggests that while it may be natural for bird and beast to prey on each other, Zeus nevertheless has a deuce in the human pack, the gift of justice (*dike*), and that crime does not, ultimately, pay – 'for justice wins over violence as they come out in the end.' Those familiar with the work of Christian theologians will recognize a hard-worked escape clause here. Hesiod was by no means the last man in an economic impasse who found himself driven to nudge divine morality a little further up the steep and rocky hill of ethics. Mapping this landscape for the average man also meant clearing up and reorganizing (in some cases bowdlerizing) the murky, archaic, often inconsistent myths regarding the gods. This task Hesiod attempted in his *Theogony*. Here he stands between the symbolic, paratactic world outlook of Homer and that subsequent struggle to achieve linear, conceptual thought (as exhilarating as it was painful) which we can see in the early Milesian philosophers (pp. 96 ff.).

The *Theogony* is a remarkable pioneering work. True, Hesiod's terms of reference are still largely non-linear; his categorizing remains at an elementary level (no distinction, for instance, between moral and non-moral); while his semi-conceptualized figures, such as Eris (Strife), are *persons* rather than personified abstractions, for the simple reason that Hesiod did not know what an abstraction was. Yet the originality and penetration of his unprecedented attempt to grapple with the real and perennial problems of life are clear from the fact that, in one way or another, the hares he started – from the dilemma of divine omniscience and divine morality to that of determinism and free will – are still running vigorously today. With Hesiod, Greek intellectual thought may be said to have begun – and in a characteristically bold manner. The ferment is now at work; the process, once set in motion, will never stop.

'Men make the polis'

One odd feature about Hesiod's work is a singular lack of reference, in the social scene he portrays, to the *polis* as a dominant force: final authority still rests with the bribe-devouring *basileis*. Yet less than a generation later evidence for *polis* rule is everywhere and unmistakable: Archilochus (*see* p. 75), writing during the first half of the seventh century, may be an individualist, but nevertheless already operates within a collective context, civic as well as military. Perhaps Hesiod's Boeotia – then as later – was a backward region; but it also seems clear that the *idea* of the city-state crystallized very fast – and in direct political response to precisely those injustices which Hesiod himself had noted in his *Works and Days*. Again and again we find it taken for granted that the main function of any *polis* is to promote justice and *eunomia* – the latter a somewhat vague concept, variously interpreted according to one's political persuasion (for conservatives it meant maintenance of the traditional *status quo*, for radicals reform), but most often translated as 'good government'.

First, though, just what *was* the *polis*? Later Greek writers had no doubts on this score. Alcaeus, writing soon after 600, said: 'it is not well-roofed houses or well-built stone walls or canals and dockyards which make a *polis*, but men able to use their opportunity'. Thucydides (*c.* 460–*c.* 400) was even more succinct: 'Men,' he said, 'make the *polis*.' Yet the *polis*, like most Greek ideas or abstractions, was concrete enough to begin with, as we have seen: a central fortress, round which huddled the (originally unwalled) *asty*, or agricultural village, with its *agora* – the 'gathering-place' where men met to exchange goods or opinions – as a secondary focal-point. But how, and why, did the *basileis* disappear from the scene with so little fuss? And how did the physical *polis* come to embody that disciplined, collective ideal which sustained the Greeks throughout the classical period – and which, indeed, they cherished long after it had become politically obsolete?

77 Right: detail of an Attic marble relief portraying an Athenian hoplite (early fifth century BC).

78, 79 Opposite: the earliest known surviving panoply of Greek hoplite armour (from Argos, *c.* 700 BC). The conical helmet resembles some Assyrian examples, and reflects Eastern influence (above). Miniature bronze group of an armourer working on a helmet (eighth century BC).

The *basileus* did not rule solely by virtue of his blood. Land and capital came into it as well, enabling him to afford the chariots, horses, weapons and armour essential for a cavalry-led feudal defence force. Above all, like a medieval baron, he had his own retainers, his ready-made private army. Originally both priest and judge for the *demos*, he had always been most valued in his capacity as their military defender, Homer's 'shepherd of the people'. Developments in the eighth and seventh centuries, however, made drastic inroads into his traditional functions and privileges. The codification of law into written records severely circumscribed his hitherto arbitrary judicial powers. The dispersal of hereditary priestly offices among a number of noble families confirms this levelling trend. The most significant development, however, datable to about 700 B C, was the emergence of the hoplite phalanx – a well-equipped, well-drilled heavy infantry force, recruited (on a part-time emergency basis) from citizens who could afford the new, cheaper, much-improved panoply now being imported from the Near East, or manufactured locally in imitation of it.

The psychological and political implications of this new civic defence force, in which farmers, merchants, well-to-do artisans and indigent aristocrats fought shoulder to shoulder for their community, were nothing short of momentous. Homeric individualism vanished overnight, and the whole concept of a chariot-borne monarch cheered on by the peasantry went with it. Most true-blue aristocrats, choosing social prestige over effective power, hived off into the small, costly, exclusive cavalry arm; since from now until Philip II's day (mid fourth century: *see* pp. 161 ff.) the issue of a battle was never decided by cavalry alone, they could no longer pose as their city's indispensable protectors. There was no democratic leveller to match the phalanx, where each man's shield defended his neighbour, and social distinctions went for nothing. The hoplites' collective achievement inspired a collective sense of pride. Here, if anywhere, we can glimpse the roots of the concept identifying the *polis* with its citizens.

This sense of collective identity was made possible by the minuscule numbers involved. With a few key exceptions (fifth-century Athens had a *voting* population of perhaps fifty to sixty thousand, while cities like Thebes or Argos varied between this figure and forty thousand over all), most Greek *poleis* were lucky if they could muster five thousand inhabitants. Space, too, was limited, often to a few square miles. Both restrictions were looked on as a virtue, and actively cultivated, since the constant *polis* ideal was direct representation for every citizen with a vote: collective concentration and, if possible – though in practice this could seldom be obtained – self-sufficiency (*autarkeia*). (Aristotle claimed that the ideal was for citizens to avoid manual labour, a characteristic prejudice on his part which does not seem to be borne out by the facts.) Justice must not only be done, but, in the most literal sense, be seen to be done, in a place of assembly where one man could, physically, address the whole enfranchised body. There must also be political unity: a mere federation of states or villages did not qualify. Nor, most important of all, did barbarians; the *polis* was an exclusively Greek phenomenon.

What general pattern emerges? A conscious working towards the machinery of collectivism, exemplified by the codification of laws, the multiplication of administrative posts, the swing against *ex officio* life appointments (though there were exceptions, *e.g.* the Areopagus Council in Athens, composed of ex-archons, or the Gerousia at Sparta), the tendency to elect officials by majority vote for a one-year tenure (as early as 683 B C in the case of the Athenian archonship), the right of free citizens to exercise that vote, and the sense of collective comradeship engendered by the hoplite phalanx. At the same time (a point less often stressed) there were various political allegiances still pulling very hard *against* all these trends, and forcing a compromise over the final structure of the *polis* in effective practical terms. Though the tribal-aristocratic pattern of society had been greatly modified, it still had enormous (and often unconscious) influence over men's minds.

The system of rival clan-based power pyramids, under a few noble families, persisted throughout the classical period: they were then known as *hetairiai* – political clubs or associations – but only the name had changed. The key administrative body was, and long remained, not the Assembly, but the Council (*Boulê*) which chose and prepared its agenda for debate. Citizen rights were always heavily weighted in favour of property-owners. Only Athenians with solid capital behind them could obtain high political office; and it is surprising how far the city's noble ruling clans (Eupatrids), even in the fifth century, maintained their near-monopoly of Attica's landed estates. Thus while the principle might have changed, the same men, in practice, continued to hold the reins of power. Furthermore, at least until Cleisthenes' reforms (*see* pp. 92–4), Athens retained the fundamentally tribal structure of the old kinship system. This encouraged local traditions and cults; more important, it left considerable *de facto* power in the hands of the local squirearchy. Clan justice, especially over such matters as the blood-feud or vendetta, ran flat counter to the notion of central government and equal justice for all men – a problem which Greece has not wholly resolved to this day.

The *idea* of the *polis*, in fact, long preceded its full implementation, just as it long survived its political obsolescence. One major key to Greek history during this period is the endless contrapuntal tension between rational progressivism and emotional conservatism, civic ideals and ties of consanguinity, blood-guilt and jury justice, old religion and new secularizing philosophy. It is this clash which provides the main dialectic underlying Greek (in effect Attic) drama, and which also lurks behind the constant polarization of *polis*-dwellers into two mutually destructive groups: the Few and the Many, oligarchs and populists, reactionaries and radicals. Cross-currents abounded; the lines were neither clearly nor neatly drawn; but the central dichotomy existed, to form a major, often a tragic, element in Greek political history. Legitimate political dissent was often hard to distinguish from treachery or pure sedition, *stasis*; and *stasis* could, all too easily, escalate into bloody civil war. Conservatives praised *eunomia* as the bulwark of the community; radicals countered with *isonomia*, equality under the law, the implementation of which produced – according to one's viewpoint – either democracy or mob rule. Somewhere between these two extreme positions the whole political history of the Greek states was hammered out.

There was also the embarrassing problem of how to reconcile this brave new civic world with archaic tribal deities who remained obstinately indifferent to human ethics. Demeter and Dionysus might suffice for the unthinking peasantry; intellectuals were scandalized to find the gods in heaven falling short of their own middle-class aspirations – and often reflecting, with uncomfortable accuracy, an all-too-human set of irresponsible, sensual, aristocratic values. To give Olympus moral tone proved far from easy: there was too great a body of well-established mythic tradition (not to mention Homer) telling quite a different story. It was left for Hesiod to set an ethical cat among the theological pigeons by making justice – in heaven as on earth – the central problem of life. How can godhead be immoral? Why do the wicked prosper? Such questions recur uncomfortably throughout Greek literature. They are with us still today.

80 The only known inscribed portrait of Hesiod, wearing fillet, chiton and cloak (fourth century AD mosaic from Trier, by Monnus). However, 'since Hesiod lived long before the concept of individualized portraiture was born in Greece, each artist was free to depict him according to his imagination' (Gisela Richter, *Portraits of the Greeks*).

81 Detail of a terracotta jug (seventh century BC) from Arkades, a Dorian town situated west of Mount Dikte, Crete. Crude technique does not lessen the cheerfully casual realism of this boy-meets-girl sketch. Sculpture from Arkades reveals a similar human interest.

82 Ivory relief from Samos (c. 630–620 BC): Perseus decapitating Medusa. The Gorgon's face is presented as a characteristic apotropaic mask, and the execution reveals obvious Oriental influence.

One dominant feature of the period 650–600 is a rapidly developing emphasis on human concerns, a progressive hominocentrism. Paradoxically, this is most apparent in the way the Greeks now treated their gods. While mere human houses remained of baked mud-brick, sometimes (though not always) on a stone base, those of the gods – and a temple was, in essence, the *house of a god* rather than a place of worship, since the altar stood outside – rapidly developed in richness and intricacy. Early shrines, which resembled nothing so much as thatched cottages, with gable roofs and smoke-holes, were replaced by more sophisticated structures, first of timber, then of dressed stone. It is no accident that their model was the Mycenaean *megaron*, with its pillared porch, antechamber and colonnade; nor that the original hearth or sacrificial pit was replaced by a lifelike cult-statue of the god, which became the temple's chief focal point. The anthropomorphizing trend is unmistakable, and confirmed by a growing stress on human motifs in seventh-century vase-painting. Gods, like the Gorgons and Chimaeras of Oriental myth, were losing their *mana* and acquiring humanity in exchange; so they had to be provided with the best (*i.e.* most traditionally royal) in the way of human lodgings.

Economically speaking, the amount invested in these elaborate non-functional buildings and the statues they contained (which largely contributed to the need for, and development of, life-size or more-than-life-size sculpture as an art form) was out of all proportion to a small city-state's standard of living, technical resources or available public funds. Why? Not, I think, religious fervour, except in a most generalized sense. The answer seems to be, rather, that this new-style temple offered an infinitely rewarding medium for the expression of civic pride and propaganda. The conscious dignity and affluence of any *polis* could be measured by the splendour of its public (which meant, primarily, its religious) architecture, thus also satisfying those – the hoplites in particular – who sought some tangible expression for their unity of purpose and achievement. The *polis* soon became an idea, or ideal, to which the temple of its patron deity gave lavish and satisfying concrete form, at once article of faith and status symbol – especially if it stood high on the acropolis, where all men could see it. Just how far the individual sank himself in the collective may be judged from the fact that henceforth the only self-aggrandizement tolerated was that of the *polis* as a whole.

Yet within these seventh-century Greek communities all was by no means well. It would be a great mistake to suppose that collectivism ironed out inequality, far less injustice. Many aristocrats, and a growing minority of middle-class entrepreneurs, might be riding high on the new post-colonial economic boom; but the introduction of the profit-and-luxury motif to a primarily agricultural society had highly disruptive long-term effects, and while some clever men with capital made a killing, many more, mostly smallholders, were going to the wall. Athens and Sparta, the two states for which we have most evidence, present somewhat anomalous features: the former, indeed, demands separate consideration (*see* pp. 71 ff.). Sparta, likewise a law to herself, in this as other matters, had very early (*c.* 675–650) avoided revolution by reorganizing her citizen body as an internally democratic power elite, with the first probouleutic council – i.e. one that prepared agenda for the Assembly – known to Greek history. This new regime retained Sparta's archaic dual kingship, and held its position by exploiting the downtrodden indigenous population of Laconia and Messenia as a permanent serf labour force.

In general, however, changing conditions tended to be symbolized by the emergence of that interesting phenomenon, the *tyrannos*. Later philosophical writers, smarting under the autocratic habits of Alex-

83, 84, 85, 86 Carvings from the sanctuary of Artemis Orthia, Sparta, *c.* 600 BC. Left to right: bone-carving of a Spartan woman, who seems to be mourning (one is reminded of the famous injunction given by such women to their men, to return either with their shields or on them); two carved bone plaques portraying Spartan warriors; and an ivory plaque representing a docked warship: 'At the stern the captain seems to be greeting a woman on landing . . . ; a seaman is fishing from the bow compartment, and on the ram another seaman appears to be relieving himself' (Morrison and Williams, *Greek Oared Ships*).

ander the Great (*see* pp. 170ff.), gave 'tyranny' the pejorative sense it still bears today; but at first a *tyrannos* was simply any non-hereditary ruler who acquired power by unconstitutional means – generally a *coup d'état*. Far from being unpopular, he more often than not owed his elevation to widespread public support. Gyges of Lydia, the earliest known *tyrannos* (the word itself is said to be Lydian in origin), had his claim endorsed, after the event, by the Delphic Oracle: a surprising blow at established tradition. Would-be Greek usurpers were not slow to take the hint. Conditions, moreover, were propitious. The vast expansion of trade and commerce had made financial backing available to all, regardless of pedigree. The hoplite phalanx now constituted a potential private army for anyone clever enough to buy or otherwise enlist its support during a factional struggle. Social disruption and economic distress had thrown up a deprived class willing to follow any leader who offered them a new deal. Many successful merchants had capital but lacked political power, and would, similarly, provide funds in return for the chance of office.

87 A Roman copy of a bust tentatively identified as the Spartan lawgiver Lycurgus; but this is doubtful, and Homer has also been suggested.

88, 89 Periander (*c.* 625–585 BC), among the most successful and striking of all Greek *tyrannoi*, is represented here by a herm found near Tivoli, bearing the inscription 'Periander of Corinth, son of Cypselus: practice is everything' (left). His great wealth largely derived from traffic across the Isthmus; his *diolkos*, or slipway (right) made it possible to haul cargo-vessels from the Saronic to the Corinthian Gulf without transhipping their freight.

From about 675 onwards, not surprisingly, *tyrannoi* began to seize power in city-states all over the Aegean world: at Argos, Sicyon, Corinth, Mytilene, Samos, Naxos, Miletus and Megara among others. One predictable common factor which all such coups reveal is a prosperous urban-commercial background. Tyrants did not make headway in under-developed areas (*e.g.* Arcadia) or cattle-baron country such as Thessaly. Nor were they a symptom of social revolution in the full sense, bourgeois and peasants united against an effete aristocracy. The power struggle remained, fundamentally, between men at the top, equals or near-equals, each supported by his faction, his social pyramid, drawn from various committed groups within the structure of the *polis*. One major secret of the success they enjoyed lay in their economic expertise, the fruits of which were duly passed on to the citizen body as a whole. It is no accident that the more successful *tyrannoi* were eager to promote fresh colonizing ventures, and even got

together to form an international trading cartel. Such men (like Cypselus of Corinth, who not only enjoyed great popularity himself, but was succeeded without incident by his even more remarkable son Periander) did not impose their will on a sullen and resentful populace. So long as they delivered the economic goods, *tyrannoi* could rely on enthusiastic support.

Athens' agrarian crisis developed comparatively late: for once she followed the field rather than leading it. Her true revolution, moreover, was postponed by conservative concessions (followed, as we shall see – pp. 88 ff. – by a delayed tyranny). The early unification of Attica had provided her with what, at the time, seemed ample *Lebensraum*. As a result she had neither sent out colonists nor encroached on her neighbours' territories. Not until about 600, in fact, when the land problem was already acute, do we find Athenians fighting for Salamis, and for Sigeum on the Hellespont. One root cause of the trouble, paradoxically, was a general improvement in living standards. Stability, as always, raised the population level, which in turn affected conditions on the farms. The old law by which all sons had a share in their father's estate worked well enough so long as even one of them was lucky to survive. But improved actuarial prospects meant that estates were broken up until the individual holdings were no longer economically viable – a fact which owner-farmers obstinately refused to recognize.

They began to plough up more (and more poor or marginal) land, which increased the danger of soil exhaustion. They fell into debt, and mortgaged their land on the security of their person: failure to meet repayments was common, and left the wretched debtor a *de facto* serf, working the land for his creditor's benefit, and paying him (probably: the evidence is ambiguous) one-sixth of each year's crop. The creditor was now sitting pretty: he could either sell the debtor into slavery for defaulting on a personally secured loan, or else keep him as a permanently obligated chattel, with no chance of getting free. To begin with, the second alternative looked more attractive; but as time went on, and wealthy aristocrats became addicted to foreign luxury goods, superfluous workers tended, more and more, to be traded off abroad against imports. A more socially inflammable practice could hardly be imagined.

Scarcely less notorious were the hated boundary-stones (*horoi*) – which Solon (*see* pp. 83 ff.) was to remove – indicating that the land was mortgaged to, or in some cases the property of, some creditor-landlord. There is no real evidence for the popular belief that property in ancient Attica could not legally be sold or transferred, and much to support Aristotle's picture of rampant speculation in real estate, with more and more land passing into the hands of a wealthy and well-connected minority. Given these conditions, some sort of political explosion became inevitable.

Yet when the first coup was attempted, it is worth noting that it failed through lack of popular support. Probably in 632, a young aristocrat named Cylon, a handsome Olympic victor, seized the Acropolis with the support of troops provided by his father-in-law Theagenes, tyrant of Megara. Far from flocking to overthrow the government, Attica's downtrodden citizens obediently besieged the rebels. When Cylon's men surrendered for lack of food and water, they were treacherously murdered by that year's archon, Megacles the Alcmaeonid, and his supporters. Delphi, having backed Cylon, now placed the whole Alcmaeonid clan under a curse, which involved their expulsion from Attica (they were very soon back, however, and intriguing as hard as ever). The whole incident points to some pretty tough in-fighting among the top noble families, with political expulsion a recognized weapon in the game. The failure of the populace to back a *prima facie* attractive rebel suggests either political cynicism (why exchange Cox for Box?) or else that in 632 agrarian conditions had by no means reached their nadir. Basically, too, no one yet thought in radical terms: the Big House feudal mentality persisted regardless. Even the subsequent advent of democratic methods did not daunt Athens' privileged aristocrats. Though in some ways they might have their wings clipped, they soon adapted themselves with easy dexterity to the new democratic power game, and very often played it better than their opponents.

90 View from the Areopagus to the Acropolis; between the two is the approximate location of the slaughter of Cylon's supporters by Megacles and his men. The rebels surrendered at discretion, and emerged from sanctuary still clinging to a rope attached to the goddess's altar. The rope snapped, whereupon Megacles, taking this as an omen, at once dispatched them.

The individual voice

Shortly after Hesiod's day we are confronted with an upsurge, throughout the Aegean world, of short, personal, intensely felt poems, by women as well as men: what we would term 'lyric verse', though to the Greeks themselves this simply denoted a piece composed for accompaniment on the lyre. Individualism is the keynote: a quality also discernible in religious developments, the politics of social protest, commercial expansion and the visual arts. Greek lyric poetry emerged during the great colonization movement, and had more or less exhausted its initial impulse by the time of the Persian Wars. During the fifth century it gave way to drama, which embodied much of its essential features in choral form, and to prose, which became the logical medium for scientific or philosophical investigation, oratory and rhetoric, and narrative history. We may therefore legitimately regard it as a characteristic feature of the age which produced it, psychologically, culturally and intellectually: a phenomenon to link up with the first stone temples, free-standing *kouroi*, the development of quasi-secular vase-painting, and the increasing tendency of artists to sign their work with their own names.

One of the most striking things about these poems is their variety. They come in strophes, couplets, quatrains or unstructured sequences. Their authors, and dialects, are drawn from every part of the Aegean world, and the range of personal attitudes they reveal is equally broad. Homeric parody and military jingoism, love poetry both homo- and heterosexual, moody autumnal pessimism about the vanity and brevity of life, animal fables, political propaganda, flyting invective, diatribes against women, paeans in praise of drink, anti-heroic satire: ego-tripping, clearly, can claim respectable archaic antecedents. Theognis apart, we have no manuscripts of these authors, famous though many of them are: merely snippets culled from grammarians or gossip-writers, and tattered papyrus fragments preserved by the dry sands of Egypt. Paradoxes abound. We have a luxury-loving Spartan poet in Alcman, and a dull prosaic Athenian one in Solon. The forms of verse employed were almost as wide-ranging. Elegy (perhaps originally a song with flute accompaniment: hexameter alternating with pentameter, and thus in a sense transitional between epic and lyric) served variously for drinking-songs, odes, laments, dedications and epitaphs. Iambics, much akin to English blank verse or Alexandrines, were popular for satirical invective: Archilochus and, later, Hipponax used them frequently. The four-line stanza, except in Sappho and Alcaeus, was comparatively rare.

For the Greeks, the true basic distinction was between monody, *i.e.* a song to be sung by one person with lyre accompaniment, and choral works performed by a choir and leader, most often with dancing as well as music. We do not know the dance-steps, and the early music is lost: all we have are the words and their rhythm. This is rather like trying to reconstruct an opera or oratorio solely from the libretto. We should also bear in mind that though all these types of lyric expression acquired literary prominence only during the seventh century, they had (like epic) existed in oral form since time immemorial, whether as public ceremony or private folk-song. Homer reveals the existence of dirges, paeans and wedding-hymns. Archilochus in his beast fables and scurrilous polemic hints at an age-old folk-tradition which surfaced in durable form only after the discovery of writing. Literacy, in general, tends to tidy up art, to organize it in respectable patterns: the man who can read and write is already half bourgeois. The drunken impromptu dithyramb in honour of Dionysus was put on a regular footing by Arion, who – besides riding dolphins – had the essentially middle-class gift of making poetry pay off in hard cash. Archaic Greece on the whole, however, tended (the Homeridae apart) to distrust literary professionalism, and it took a couple of fifth-century

91 Arion astride a dolphin, holding a lyre: reverse of bronze coin from Methymna, second–first century BC.

92 The 'Mnesiepean Inscription' relating to Archilochus, on Paros: set up c. 250 BC by Mnesiepes in a shrine dedicated to the poet, and devoted to his life and work. The remaining fragments were discovered and edited in 1952 by N. M. Kontoléon.

giants – Simonides and Pindar – to legitimize the idea of a poet, like anyone else, being worthy of his hire.

The first lyric poet known to us, Archilochus (?716–c. 650) is also one of the most memorable. An aggressive individualist, wryly sardonic in his attitude to the world around him, he packed his spare verse with brilliant, disconcertingly realistic imagery and a biting blend of sensuousness and satire. Born on barren Paros, the illegitimate son of an aristocrat and a slave-woman, he joined the earliest colonizing expedition to Thasos, off the Thracian coast – and provides us with priceless evidence, in his work, of seventh-century frontier life. Always in danger from Thracian tribesmen or rival prospectors – like the Klondike, Thasos had its gold-rush – the settler enjoyed few consolations save whoring and drinking. All this Archilochus sets down, without heroics, in phrases as vivid as any Japanese *haiku*. He spares neither himself (we hear a lot about his impotence), nor his friends (such as the dandified Glaucus, whose gravestone turned up a few years ago), nor the unlucky girl he never quite managed to marry. His

93 The original epitaph of Glaucus, Archilochus' fellow colonist on Thasos (where the gravestone was found). It reads: 'Glaucus son of Leptines am I: the sons of Brentis set me up'.

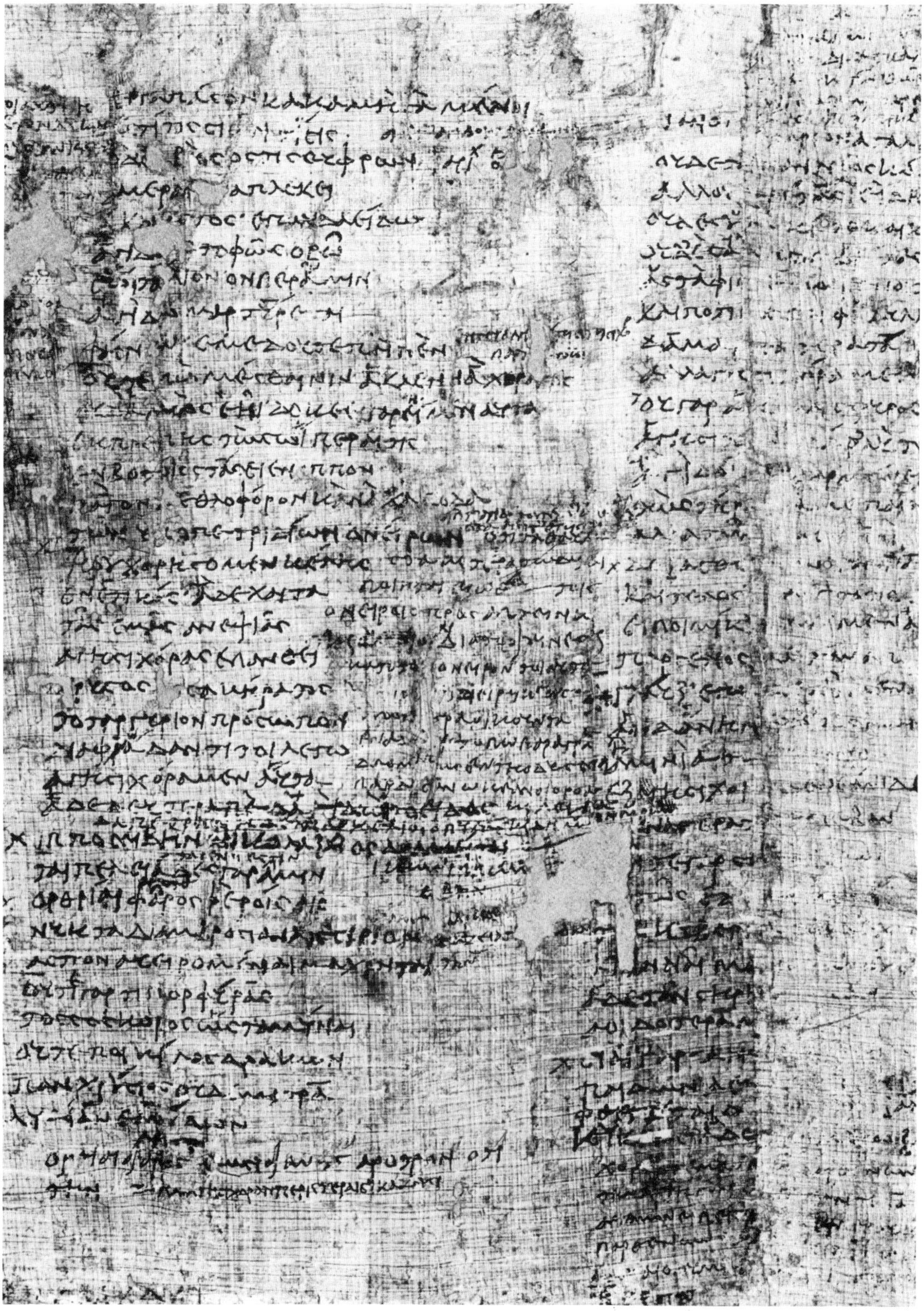

broken engagement to Neobule, indeed, sparked off some of his most vitriolic invective. No less serious a poet than Homer (so they judged him in antiquity), yet the most un-Homeric of old soldiers, he describes the skirmishes of love and war with an equally unromantic eye. In Archilochus, Thersites has come of age.

Other near-contemporary poets – Callinus of Ephesus, Tyrtaeus and Terpander at Sparta – could still, without self-consciousness, and inspired by the new *polis* ideal, hit an almost Kiplingesque note of parish patriotism. If Archilochus is the colonists' poet, these show us the collective hoplite ethic in action. Chariots and individual prowess are out, and war has become (as it was long to remain) a kind of bloodier football match, where you stood in line and shoved until something gave. Yet even at Sparta, in the seventh century, there was still room for a learned, frivolous and frankly eccentric poet such as Alcman, whose famous *Partheneion* (maiden-song), partly preserved on papyrus, shows us a complex and luxurious world, as remote as could well be imagined from the later stereotype of crude Spartan militarism. This is not to say that political conditions had no impact on a poet's outlook or imagery. When Gyges of Lydia occupied Colophon – hitherto among the most powerful of Ionian cities – its inhabitants lost their civic self-confidence, retreating into mere private hedonism. Such a mood is perfectly reflected by that nostalgic pessi-mist Mimnermus – himself a Colophonian – whose autumnal imagery of inexorable, melancholy decay, the fading life-cycle, forms one highly characteristic leitmotiv in Greek lyric poetry. Equally typical are those odd tirades against women which (in more than one sense) likewise symbolize man's sense of anxiety, impotence and frustration.

As conditions became more settled, however, and men gained further control over their environment, such imagery gradually faded into the background. In particular, we find less recurrent emphasis on the omnipotence of Zeus as a kind of fatalistic shorthand term for the absolute helplessness of the individual. 'Hope and self-persuasion,' Semonides of Amorgos noted, with wry accuracy, 'keep us all alive in our unprofitable desires.' Of no poets was this truer, in their very different ways, than Alcaeus and Sappho – both aristocrats from the island of Lesbos, and both roughly datable to the period 620–570. Like Theognis a century later (*see* p. 102), Alcaeus reveals himself as a right-wing diehard, homosexual by temperament and brim-ming with political bile. To him we owe (along with various choice insults, mostly directed at his bugbear Pittacus) the first known appearance of the 'Ship of State' metaphor in European poetry. In exile he seems to have derived his main consolation from the wine-jar – a resentful casualty of the new mercantile world which had so brusquely

94 Opposite: papyrus of Alcman's *Partheneion* (col. ii): *c*. AD 50, from Memphis (Saq-qara). Written in an edu-cated, cursive hand: probably 'a copy made for a scholar for his personal use' (Turner, *Greek Manuscripts*).

95 Stylized representation of Sappho and Alcaeus on a *kalathos-psykter* (wine-cooler) by the school of the Brygos Painter (from Acragas, the modern Agrigento, 480–470 BC); both hold a lyre and plectrum.

by-passed him and his old-fashioned, not to say reactionary, beliefs. A landed squire *manqué*, he had an equally appreciative eye for long-tailed widgeon and pretty boys: the final paradoxical impression he gives is of Hilaire Belloc rewritten by Cavafy.

Yet the fame of Alcaeus (as of Archilochus before him) was ultimately eclipsed by that of a woman: small, dark, not very good-looking, and perhaps in some way crippled. Sappho's life was largely absorbed by her private relationships and the pursuit of beauty. Her poetry reflects, not those political cross-currents in which she so nearly drowned – like Alcaeus she was twice exiled – but, first and foremost, her intense attachments to various girls, who formed a kind of circle (*thiasos*) round her. The fierce gales of Lesbos, characteristically, she used as a symbol for her own violent passions: no doubt about the order of priorities there. Sappho's poetry tells us rather less about revolution on Lesbos than Jane Austen's novels reveal concerning the Napoleonic Wars. The bulk of her surviving poems and fragments, no more than one-twentieth of what she actually wrote, deal with her love-affairs and emotional crises, to the virtual exclusion of everything else. Even when she introduces a mythical theme, it tends to be as a gloss on some current private relationship. Here we have the individual voice yet again, this time in an extraordinarily modern guise. Sappho is currently (1972) enjoying a campus cult in American universities. It is not hard to see why.

One remarkable, indeed unique, feature of her work which must be counted an important factor in explaining her popularity today, is a blessed freedom from sexual shame or guilt, a blazing aristocratic assumption of rightness and beauty in all her relationships. We see here, as nowhere else, that strange spring interlude between the successive (though very different) collectivisms of Homeric society and the city-state. Such exclusive emphasis on private life and personal preoccupations would not recur again until the Hellenistic Age, after Alexander's death. To Pericles and his fifth-century contemporaries the private individual, or *idiotes*, was an idiot in our modern sense, irresponsible because unconcerned with public affairs. Aesthetics, however, have had the last laugh. Great literature need not be public – or, indeed, responsible. Sappho's clear yet close-wrought imagery, her feeling for the *mot juste*, the emotionally heightened charge with which she can load a seemingly simple quatrain – all testify to her crystalline, timeless genius. The glimpses she offers of her tiny, intense, sunlit, suffering world are, oddly, more real than Alcaeus' political attitudinizing: they have the sensuous clarity of a Minoan fresco. If Sappho transcends the pleasure principle, she also makes Women's Lib look like a crutch for middle-class misfits. The moral is worth pondering.

96 A papyrus fragment (second century AD) containing the end of Book I of Sappho's poems: the text notes that this book contained 1,320 lines. Only a few words are preserved legibly: 'Maidens... all night long . . . singing . . . breast violet-sweet . . . rise up . . . go with your . . . where so much . . . we shall see sleep . . .'.

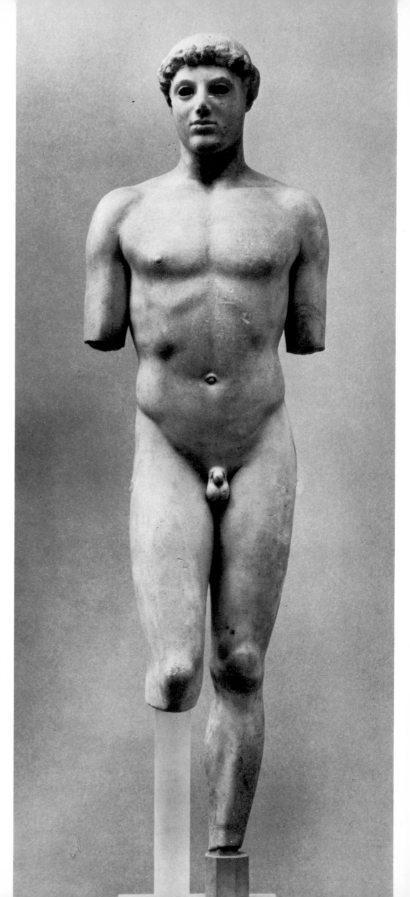

97 The 'Critios Boy' or 'Ephebe of Critios' (Acropolis, Athens, 490–480 BC) portrays, it has been suggested, a victor in the Panathenaic Festival. The attribution to Critios (co-author with Nesiotes of the bronze 'Tyrannicide Group') is uncertain. Lullies (*Greek Sculpture*) calls it 'a splendid example of the new distribution of weight which was a precondition for the perfectly poised Classical figure'.

80

3
Reason, tradition and
the Persian Wars (600–479 B C)

Solon and the Athenian economy

During the sixth century B C and the first two decades of the fifth, Greece's great revolution in thought, culture, art and politics was finally brought to completion. The distance travelled can be seen, almost at a glance, in the development of those standing male statues known as *kouroi*. With the passage of time their original Egyptian stance begins to lose its stiff and hieratic formality. Though still primarily concerned with an abstract ideal rather than any sort of realistic representation, Greek artists are acquiring some knowledge of anatomy, some acquaintance with the basic relationship between bone and muscle. Then, almost with the abruptness of a mutation, after Marathon (490) but before Salamis (480), comes the so-called 'Ephebe of Critios', rightly described by Lord Clark as 'the first beautiful nude in art'. The passion for mathematical precision has not been lost, but now it is married to a flowering sensuous awareness, a delight in the naked athleticism of the trained male body. The whole cultural and political breakthrough is implicit in that achievement; the Idea has been made manifest in flesh.

Politically, the age is most remarkable for two things: the slow, painful, hit-and-miss evolution of democratic government at Athens, and the steady rise of Persia as a great imperial power, dominating the Near and Middle East from Mesopotamia to the Black Sea, absorbing the Ionian littoral, and – under Darius I – reaching out exploratory tentacles into Europe (514/3). From now on these two phenomena, hitherto independent of one another, were drawn inexorably on to collision course. It may well be that the final clash between Persia and the Greek states (490–479) acted as a catalyst for that Greek sense of pride and independence which reached its dazzling

98 Obverse of Persian silver shekel (*siglos*), *c.* 485–450 BC, showing the Great King with bow and arrow. Twenty *sigloi* were the equivalent of a gold daric.

81

zenith during the mid fifth century. The psychological effect of standing off this mighty barbarian host was incalculable. Changes in art, thought and political outlook had long been maturing; but it may well have been that the tensions of conflict, the great triumph against seemingly impossible odds, did much to precipitate the transition. At all events, it is against that background of crisis and ultimate victory that the scholars' labels are changed, and 'archaic' Greece finally becomes 'classical'. Though in many ways less than definable, this metamorphosis is one of profound importance.

What is often referred to, misleadingly, as the 'birth of democracy' – an instantaneous event, one is made to feel, if not actually from Zeus' head – was in fact a protracted and painful accouchement which demanded, and eventually got, Caesarean section. It began with Solon's stop-gap legislation (?573/2; *see* Miller, Bibliography) and culminated in the reforms of Cleisthenes (507/6). It thus remains not only a sixth-century phenomenon, but an exclusively Athenian one. We have already studied the mounting agrarian crisis in Attica (*see* p. 71); with landowners increasingly prone to sell off debt-bondsmen into slavery as a quick means of raising capital, social unrest had grown

99 Detail of an amphora, showing a mounted warrior, in full panoply, accompanied by his squire (foreground), who has carefully dressed long hair and wears a short-sleeved purple chiton (attributed to Lydos, *c.* 540 BC).

a good deal more acute since Cylon's day. Revolution was in the air: the widening gap between haves and have-nots polarized and exacer-bated extreme attitudes. While wealthy Eupatrids called for bloody repression, the peasantry demanded redistribution of Attica's limited farming land. By the mid 570s so hopeless – and dangerous – a dead-lock had been reached that both sides expressed their readiness to accept arbitration as a preferable alternative to endless factionalism, civil war or the 'strong man' solution of tyranny.

The mediator chosen was a moderately well-off Eupatrid named Solon, who as a young man had gone into trade, and thus stood some-what outside the great land debate. A few years before, he had also urged, and perhaps led, the expedition which secured Salamis as Athenian territory. His business background gave him a flair for economics unusual in men of his class, combined, improbably, with an old-fashioned aristocratic moral code. Thus though he saw, very clearly, that one of Athens' major weaknesses was an inadequate export balance, he also (like most financially innocent reactionaries) regarded the abuse of wealth as the root of all evil. This view, of course, he shared with almost everyone in Athens except the more

100 Transport of grain by means of mules: detail from an Attic-style black-figure cup (sixth century BC).

101 Detail of a black-figure cup by Nikosthenes (from Vulci, sixth century BC) show-ing ploughing and sowing.

successful landowners. It is not hard to see how all parties convinced themselves that this was the man to look after their particular interests. For the Eupatrids he was one of themselves, and would (they argued) operate on the principle of *noblesse oblige*. The rural poor, who had heard him deliver soapbox tirades in the Agora on rapacious speculation, looked forward to a radical landredistribution scheme. Both were in for something of a disappointment: Solon may well have thrown out encouraging hints all round simply in order to guarantee himself, *qua* arbitrator, solid endorsement before the event. The only group (perhaps not coincidentally) to derive solid and permanent benefit from his legislation was that to which Solon himself belonged: the merchants and traders, the welltodo new middle class operating on mobile capital rather than living off their estates.

Solon's reforms fell into three distinct categories. (When considering these we should remember that Greek statesmen, unlike their Roman successors, drew no hardandfast line between public and private law, or indeed between legal and constitutional matters generally.) First, there were his emergency measures to deal with the immediate crisis, the socalled *seisachtheia*, or 'shaking off of burdens'. He cancelled all agricultural debts and destroyed the mortgagestones set up on property, so that the creditors' rights were summarily annulled. All Athenians sold into slavery, whether at home or abroad, as well as those exiled through destitution, were to be fetched back. Loans could no longer be contracted on the security of the person: from now on we find no clearcut instance in Athenian history of a free man being enslaved, or even imprisoned, simply for debt.

An admirable programme – especially when we recall how recently many civilized countries, England included, did away with debtors' gaols; but one would dearly like to know just how it was implemented. What steps were taken to track down those abroad? More important, who paid for their release? The state lacked adequate funds; presumably their exowners were required to foot the bill, which can scarcely have pleased them. To redistribute their lands as well would have been asking for trouble at the top, and here Solon wisely let well alone, though his decision dashed all the landless majority's hopes. He thus contrived to antagonize both sides at once, and stood there (as he wrote of himself) 'like a wolf hemmed in by a pack of hounds'. Anyone who has ever seen the crowd of petitioners outside a precoup modern Greek Prime Minister's office will at once recognize the accuracy of this description.

Though by far the best known of Solon's reforms, the *seisachtheia* (which defused a specific crisis, but did little to prevent its recurrence) had no lasting significance except as a historical curiosity. Other measures, less publicized, were crucial to Athens' future development.

102 Bust tentatively identified as Solon: no reliable portrait has survived, so such identification must remain flimsy, at best.

Solon established a People's Court, the Heliaea, and gave every citizen the right to bring a prosecution. Most important of all was his constitutional redefinition of the Athenian class structure, in terms which made capital (rather than birth) the new criterion for a citizen's civil or military status. The old categories of Eupatrids, Farmers and Craftsmen were replaced by four groups based on the estimated annual yield of a man's land. Eligibility for office was still restricted (*e.g.* only the top two groups could hold the archonship), but at least the point had been made that in an era of expanding commerce, aristocratic privilege no longer offered an adequate basis for government. The days of the Big House economy were numbered. Cash, ultimately, was to prove more potent than blood – a theme on which conservative poets like Theognis (*see* p. 58) harped with melancholy persistence during the years to come. In economic terms, Solon had taken an essential step towards bringing Athens into line with the modern world.

This is equally apparent from many of his other reforms. He made it obligatory for every man to teach his son a trade – thus acknowledging the fact that Athens lacked exportable goods, and had to acquire technical skills to help pay for what she bought abroad, grain in particular. He banned the export of all produce save olive oil, a clear bid to stop rich landowners profiteering on foreign sales at the expense of the home market. He offered attractive conditions, including

103 Detail of an Attic black-figure amphora, showing men weighing merchandise on a balance-scale (*c.* 550–530 BC: said to be from Agrigento, Sicily).

citizenship, to any skilled craftsmen who would settle in Athens: within a few decades Athenian potters had eclipsed those of Corinth. Yet despite his economic insight, Solon remained a social conservative. Having redefined the class structure he attempted to freeze it as it stood. Much of his private legislation (in particular that to do with heiresses and adoption) was aimed at protecting blood and property and family. Though he had extended eligibility for office, he did not tinker with the old tribal-aristocratic power structure, which still retained its Mafia-like network of local clan-based allegiances. This, in the last resort, was what made his reforms politically unworkable: too many ambitious country squires squabbling over a dangerously under-centralized administration. In this crucial sphere Solon's Eupatrid heart had won out over his economically progressive head. The error of judgment was to prove expensive.

104–112 A group of scenes showing craftsmen at work. On this page, right: a terracotta group of women kneading bread (Boeotia, fifth century BC); detail of an Attic black-figure skyphos showing an oil-press (sixth–fifth century BC); a cobbler at work, detail of a red-figure Athenian kylix (fifth century BC); and a boy fishing, detail of a red-figure kylix (480 BC). Opposite, above and centre left, two details from fifth-century BC red-figure vases: smiths at work, and Athena modelling a horse in clay, the first stage in making a bronze statue. Opposite, centre right, and below left and right, three stages in pottery: clay being dug out (Corinthian terracotta plaque, seventh–sixth century BC), a potter making pots (vase, early fifth century BC), and pots being fired in a kiln (detail from an Athenian black-figure vase, late sixth century BC).

From Peisistratus to Cleisthenes

After promulgating his reforms, Solon went abroad for ten years. Many Athenians had hoped to see him embark on a kind of benevolent tyranny, something Solon himself was determined at all costs to avoid. The chaos that followed his departure made a 'strong man' solution look ever more tempting as time went by. Three main factions arose in the City Assembly, all led by aristocrats, and loosely connected with regional areas, whence their names: those of the Plain, the Coast, and the Hills. Twice during the next decade the archon-list was inscribed *anarchia*, 'no archon elected', probably because of rioting at the polls. One archon, a still more ominous sign, held office, illegally, for over two years before his forcible removal. When Solon returned to Athens, he found the threat of tyranny imminent, and vainly warned his fellow countrymen against it – vainly, because at this stage no one could envisage a better way of attaining reform than through authoritarian *Diktat*. A radical restructuring of society in accordance with the new *polis* outlook was still, almost literally, unthinkable.

113 Small archaic bronze of Athena Promachos (*c.* early sixth century BC). 'Promachos' is a title of Athena's as champion or defender, mostly associated with the famous 'Bronze Athena' by Pheidias, so large that seamen could glimpse its helmet as they sailed up from Sunium.

The strong man duly appeared: an aristocrat named Peisistratus, Solon's own kinsman, leader of the mixed third-estate Hill faction. In 561/0 he tricked the Assembly into voting him a bodyguard, with the help of whom he promptly seized the Acropolis. His position at first was insecure, to say the least of it: twice during the next two decades a combination of Plain and Coast removed him from office, finally driving him out of Attica. By the time he made his final comeback, in 546, he had learnt the basic formula for safe one-man rule: get solid financial reserves, and use these, *inter alia*, to buy a private army. While in exile Peisistratus had established rich Thracian mining concessions, and acquired a Scythian bodyguard (later converted into Athens' permanent police force). Thus equipped he came back, routed a citizen-levy sent out against him, and set about his long-term scheme for the civic development of Athens. He died in 528/7, and handed over power without incident to his two sons, Hippias and Hipparchus. Paradoxically, when we reflect on its totalitarian nature, his reign was looked back on afterwards, even by good democrats, as a kind of Golden Age on earth.

He saw, very clearly, that one key to the problem lay in political, civic, social and religious centralization. The job had already been done, in myth and theory, by Theseus, who was credited with the unification (*synoikismos*) of Attica into a single state, ruled from Athens. The true *synoikismos* was the work of Peisistratus. Aware that Solon's economic development programme had stalled one crisis only to start another – capitalists eager for political office, failed smallholders drifting citywards and forming an urban proletariat – the new dictator set out to save Athens by what today might be termed stop-

and-go legislation. His one-man rule clamped a kind of moratorium on constitutional development. He claimed to be maintaining Solon's laws, but did so by the simple device of packing Council and Assembly with his own nominees. Stick and carrot were applied in turn. Peisistratus' back-to-the-land movement (which he encouraged by means of long-term loans to small farmers) also aimed to stop the drift of troublemakers into Athens. Many urban breadliners were forcibly deported to rural areas. The appointment of travelling circuit judges relieved congestion in the city courts, while at the same time stripping power from local magnates who had hitherto presided over their own bench. Through these measures Peisistratus aimed at neutralizing the classic opposition pattern in Attica: groups of local factions, led by aristocratic families, each commanding its bloc vote. This was the way he himself had won power, and he had no intention of letting anyone else turn the same trick on him. To a large extent he succeeded, but his remedies were *ad hoc* only; they never got to the root of the disease.

It was Peisistratus' economic, social and civic-religious innovations which – like Solon's – had most long-term effects, and also set a pattern for the democratic leaders who succeeded him. Like many tyrants, he initiated a large public works scheme, partly as good *polis* propaganda, partly to defuse opposition by mopping up a core of urban unemployment. He placed great emphasis on the cult of Athena (again, at the expense of local heroes), building a new temple

114 Extant foundations of the so-called 'Ancient Temple' of Athena Polias, sometimes de-scribed, after its excavator, as the 'Doerpfeld Foundation'. It seems to have been first built early in the sixth century BC, and then enlarged or rebuilt, in Archaic Doric, by the Peisistratids. This view is from the south, looking northwards across the Acropolis towards the Erechtheum (in the back-ground).

115, 116 Below: the 'Peplos' *Kore* (*c.* 550–525 BC), so called because of her severe Doric robe (*peplos*), probably by the sculptor who executed the 'Rampin Horseman' (detail, right), a marble rider found on the Acropolis.

117, 118 Opposite, above: the Calf-bearer or Moschophoros (570 BC), the earliest Attic statue, apart from the 'Rampin Horseman', from the Acropolis. The pose set a long-lasting iconographic pattern. Below: a marble head thought to represent Peisistratus.

to her on the Acropolis and much embellishing that quadrennial festival known as the Greater Panathenaea, which attracted visitors from all over Greece. Either he or his sons developed the famous Athenian four-drachma pieces (tetradrachms) bearing Athena's head and sacred owl. The focus throughout was on Athens, and Athens' patron goddess. Cult-organization went hand in hand with civic improvement schemes – public gardens like the Lyceum, an improved water-supply, state pensions for veterans. Peisistratus not only organized festivals and processions; he also encouraged the beginnings of drama, and made poetic recitals an integral feature of public life. The main elements we associate with classical Athens were being established – piquant paradox – by a rich dictator who could afford heavy cultural investments without any immediate or tangible returns. Healthy international trade (and some fresh colonizing) coupled with active promotion of the arts made a dynamic formula. Temple-building flourished. In sculpture – as exemplified by the Rampin Horseman, the Peplos Kore (probably both by the same hand) and

the Calf-Bearer, or Moschophoros, a named portrait without mythical or divine attributes – we see the upsurge of a controlled but unmistakable naturalism. More intriguing still is the so-called 'Sabouroff Head', a highly idiosyncratic work in marble, with short-cropped hair and beard 'carved in low relief with hammer and point and then covered with painted stucco' (Charbonneaux, Martin and Villard, p. 151): this, it has been plausibly argued, may well portray Peisistratus himself.

During the middle decades of the sixth century it is hard to lay down any clear-cut distinctions between religion, art and propaganda. To take one obvious example: Peisistratus may have encouraged the worship of Dionysus to canalize popular emotionalism along harmless lines – religion, if not the opium of the people, at least their alcohol – but this festival also threw up, as a kind of inspired by-product, Attic tragedy and comedy. The first emergence of an actor, as distinct from the chorus, is associated with the name of Thespis, and dated to 534 B C.

Peisistratus' legacy of centralization, though fundamental, had its dangerous side: by equating Attica with Athens he started a tendency to develop the city at the expense of the rural outback. Despite his awareness of the need to break the old clan pattern once and for all, the running of local affairs was still very much monopolized by aristocratic squires. On a pragmatic level Peisistratus delivered the goods – while conditions remained favourable. The constitutional dilemma he never solved, and even his expanding economy was more fragile than it looked. It was left for the Alcmaeonid leader Cleisthenes (not altogether by deliberate intention) to grasp the nettle of tribally based government and destroy it root if not branch. The insecure foundations of the Peisistratid regime were made painfully clear during the period 520–510, when Darius I of Persia embarked on a new aggressive foreign policy in the Aegean, imposing restraints on Ionian commerce and penetrating as far as the Danube. The immediate result was a trade recession, which in turn affected the political set-up at Athens. Few dictatorships thrive on a slump. In 514 one of Peisistratus' sons, Hipparchus, was assassinated, and the survivor, Hippias, became cruel and repressive through fear. After two unsuccessful attempts to oust him – with the Delphic Oracle's encouragement – Cleisthenes finally gained his objective by bringing in King Cleomenes of Sparta (510). Hippias retired into exile at Sigeum on the Hellespont, and for two years Athens once again enjoyed the cut-throat pleasures of free, or anarchic, factionalism, as Cleisthenes and his conservative opponent Isagoras struggled for control of the government.

During this period Cleisthenes' faction consistently got the worst of it, which suggests that he had not, as yet, dreamed up his great democratic scheme for the people's benefit. At the 508 elections Isagoras secured the archonship; upon which, says Aristotle, Cleisthenes, 'being worsted in the political factions, won over the *demos* by giving away the *politeia* to the multitude'. *Politeia* here is ambiguous: it *may* mean no more than 'rule of the state', but more probably signifies 'citizenship'. Isagoras, scared that the conservatives would be swamped by a tide of newly enfranchised plebeians, called in King Cleomenes again. The Spartan's Draconian behaviour (he dissolved Solon's Assembly and banished some seven hundred families, the Alcmaeonids included) brought about an angry riot. He and his men were blockaded on the Acropolis, where presently lack of food and water forced them to surrender. The Spartans were granted a safe-conduct, and smuggled Isagoras out with them (but not his wretched supporters, who were afterwards purged). Cleisthenes came back in triumph, and proceeded to implement his great reform scheme. It was, indeed, urgently needed.

119 Opposite, above: Athenians voting, a red-figure kylix by the Brygos Painter, from Vulci (late sixth century BC).

120 Opposite, below: view of the Pnyx, Athens. Until 404/3 BC this debating area (somewhat like a Greek theatre in shape) faced north, with a view of the city. Then it was rebuilt and reversed to face south. In 330–326 BC this second version was enlarged: the photograph shows the speaker's platform (*bema*) of the third period.

Monopoly of power, it was clear, would no longer work: there had to be some consent by the governed. Every free man, landless or not, now had the right to vote. The Assembly had acquired sovereign status. It is unlikely that Cleisthenes understood the full implications of what he was doing: he was an aristocrat, and despite his radical reforms, he always continued to think in terms of rival power blocs. Nor did he intend to attack cult or kinship groups. He saw that the tribal structure must be *politically* revised, if only to put down local separatism and dynastic rivalries – but he apparently felt he could do this and still leave its socio-cultural aspects intact (to some extent, amazingly, he was right). His key idea was to substitute *neighbourhood*

for tribe or clan as the main determinant in Attica's social grouping. Attica was now divided into about 170 demes, or parish boroughs, each with its own local assembly, treasury and mayor (*demarchos*). From now on every citizen was inscribed on the electoral roll of his deme, and signed his name with his 'demotic' rather than his patronymic. Even if his descendants changed their residence, they kept the same demotic label.

But this was by no means the end of the matter. Cleisthenes at one stroke abolished the four old Ionian tribes, and replaced them with ten new ones, named after various Attic heroes. These tribes formed his basic administrative and military units: their composition is of some interest. Cleisthenes divided the demes into three groups: coastal, urban and inland. Each of the ten tribes was then allotted demes *from all three regions* (in each tribe the demes from one region were known as a *trittys*, or 'third'). Put another way, some 170 demes were divided into thirty (3 × 10) *trittyes*, which were split among the ten tribes on the basis of three to each: one coastal, one inland, one urban. Thus the tribes were not built up on a regional basis at all. Each contained a representative cross-section of the whole population, a device which broke up clan and local allegiances completely, and created a new foundation for *polis* loyalty. The Athenian citizen-levy was similarly brigaded from these ten cross-sectioned tribes, now remustered as regiments – a move which effectively met any threat of insurrection or clan-inspired civil war.

Administratively, the new tribes also provided a framework for Cleisthenes' new Council of Five Hundred. While in the Assembly each man voted on his own, the Council operated through ten rotating tribal contingents, or prytanies, of fifty each. These presided in turn, as a steering committee, for one-tenth of the year, *i.e.* on average thirty-six days. Lots were drawn daily for a President, or Duty Officer, who for twenty-four hours held the city keys and exercised supreme power. Thus most citizens during their lifetime would participate in the actual business of government. Old traditions of clan and phratry could be preserved at deme level, where they did no one any harm. When it came to the major offices of state (even though Solon's class restrictions still governed eligibility) the traditional pattern had been destroyed for ever. Rank persisted, but as a social rather than a political phenomenon. From now on the *polis* itself became the hub and centre of state affairs, and the Council of Five Hundred the *de facto* governing body. Though aristocrats continued, more often than not, to occupy posts such as the archonship, they were now accountable to their electors – who took some pleasure in reminding them of the fact. Athenian democracy had, at last, come of age.

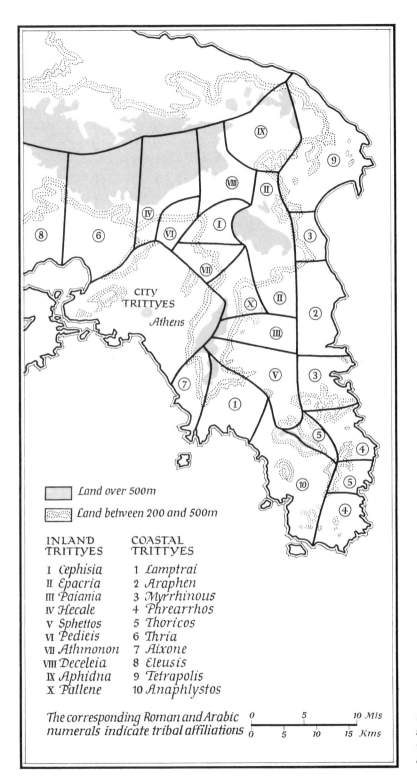

CITY
TRITTYES

Athens

Land over 500m

Land between 200 and 500m

INLAND TRITTYES	COASTAL TRITTYES
I *Cephisia*	1 *Lamptrai*
II *Epacria*	2 *Araphen*
III *Paiania*	3 *Myrrhinous*
IV *Hecale*	4 *Phrearrhos*
V *Sphettos*	5 *Thoricos*
VI *Pedieis*	6 *Thria*
VII *Athmonon*	7 *Aixone*
VIII *Deceleia*	8 *Eleusis*
IX *Aphidna*	9 *Tetrapolis*
X *Pallene*	10 *Anaphlystos*

The corresponding Roman and Arabic numerals indicate tribal affiliations

0   5   10 Mls
0   5   10   15 Kms

121 The coastal and inland *trittyes* of Attica. Some names and some boundaries are still uncertain or the subject of debate.

122 Ionian silver tetradrachm (fourth century; possibly struck by Memnon of Rhodes *c.* 336 BC). The reverse, here shown, presents 'a relief map showing the hinterland of Ephesus'. It is thus 'the earliest Greek map to come down to us in any form and the first physical relief map known' (A.E.M. Johnston, *JHS* 87, 1967). Note the loop of the Tmolus and Messogis ranges, separated by the Cayster Valley. To the north, the Hermus River; to the south, the Maeander, both flowing east–west.

Intellectual revolution: Ionia and the West

There is a curious simultaneity about the emergence of revolutionary thinkers in the ancient world. Zoroaster in Persia, Anaximander and Heracleitus in Ionian Greece, Confucius in China and Gautama Buddha in India were all near-contemporaries. It is also clear that the process of this thought involved two main streams: the scientific-philosophical and the mystical-religious. Sometimes, as in the case of Pythagoras, they overlapped; more often they were either complementary or even in opposition, catering to different sides of the human psyche. In Greece especially, the marked hominocentric trend towards secular rationalizing thought evoked an equally strong impulse to embrace some kind of mystical or transcendental belief – an impulse which neither philosophy nor the domesticated and propaganda-ridden Olympian cults could adequately satisfy. Historically, one movement preceded the other. The predominantly scientific efflorescence during the first half of the sixth century, based on Miletus and associated with the names of Thales, Anaximander and Anaximenes, gave way between 550 and 500 to a more mystically oriented movement, to which Pythagoras, Heracleitus and Xenophanes each contributed.

It was the Persians who provided a kind of axis-point between the two trends, in the years 546–539, by their conquest and occupation of Ionia and Babylon under Cyrus the Great. Exploration of the natural world, extension of man's mastery over matter, the exhilarated if naive belief that mind, alone, could solve any problem – this mood of optimism and reason soon began to crumble under the pressure of external events. Mysticism invaded mathematics; even more suggestive was the later attempt by Parmenides of Elea (*c.* 460) to prove that essential change in matter was impossible, a scientifically retrograde but all-too-influential proposition. From here it was no more than a step to Plato's equally anti-scientific notion of a permanent changeless world of Forms behind our deceptive human appearances. The psychological motivation here is clear enough. Just as the mystery cults promised salvation in the next world (above all for the socially or spiritually deprived) because the prospects in this world were so bleak, so the urge to discover an intangible, stable pattern, or model, behind the appearances was to a great extent dictated by the appalling instability of the world in which these thinkers lived.

During the first half of the sixth century the Milesians had developed something approaching a stable society: cosmopolitan, wealthy, based on widespread international trade. Such calm never endured for long in Greek city-state life, however, and Miletus was no exception. An appalling upsurge of internecine feuding (*stasis*) between the factions of Wealth (*Ploutis*) and Labour (*Cheiromacha*), in which both sides committed the most hideous atrocities, was followed, from 546 onwards, by Cyrus' piecemeal conquest of the whole Ionian littoral. Several Ionian thinkers, such as Xenophanes of Colophon, fled to the west (in particular to Sicily or southern Italy) rather than live under Persian rule. The reaction and pessimism detectable in many late thinkers, their swing away from natural science towards mystical absolutism, may well have been influenced by these political events. All things are in flux, was Heracleitus' view: that proposition simply acknowledged the observable facts of life. To posit an immanent or eternal reality behind the flux was compensatory wishful thinking. It is significant that even someone like Xenophanes, who took a very sceptical, Voltairean attitude to traditional myths concerning the gods, did so more through a preoccupation with monotheism than out of scientific curiosity.

Yet even here a note of doubt creeps in. We possess so little of what these early thinkers said or wrote, and much of that little is ambiguous. The enigma is symbolized to perfection by that famous if baffling phenomenon, the Archaic Smile. No expression more clearly and immediately identifies any sixth-century statue. Probably Anatolian in origin, by about 550 the Smile had spread over most of the Aegean world – only to disappear again, rather like the Cheshire Cat's grin, during the age that followed, when high *polis* seriousness became the fashion. No one really knows what the Archaic Smile was all about, though it has confidently been held to symbolize anything from man's divine spark to a happy extroversion supposedly typical of the Lyric Age. All we know for certain is that its natural centre of gravity lay in Ionia; and Ionia was where the conceptual, as opposed to the purely political, thinking was going on. A smile of secret and privileged knowledge, perhaps, such as Thales might have worn while meditating on water as the primal substance?

Yet Thales was also a practical sage and man of affairs. He advised the various Ionian city-states to federate, an excellent suggestion which, if followed, might have had far-reaching consequences. He was credited with diverting the River Halys for Croesus; and (whether by luck or good judgment) he predicted an eclipse. Like Solon, he was afterwards numbered among the Seven Sages, who earned that title not so much by philosophical or ethical wisdom as through statesmanship. Dicaearchus of Messene said they were *nomothetikous*, endowed with understanding 'of a lawmaking sort', and that about sums it up. They were, in fact, commemorated for having helped to nurse Greek society through that difficult stage of transition between the old tribal and the new civic ways. They were the midwives of the *polis* ideal. It is important to note that their civilization was still relatively *undifferentiated*: that is, one in which the political, philosophical,

123 Statue from Gortyn, Crete, tentatively identified (not least because of the club, an unusual adjunct) as Heracleitus. The type recalls the fifth–fourth centuries BC iconography of Asclepius.

religious, cultural, historical and scientific fields were not, as yet, clearly separated off in the minds even of its leading thinkers. No accident, surely, that sixth-century Ionia began with speculation about natural and divine phenomena, and ended (499–494) with a full-scale revolt against Persian domination. The two things were intimately linked.

The cultivation of an anti-authoritarian, reasonable, humanistic outlook on life is not something that operates in selective patches: it affects the whole cosmos. Criticism of the irrational will apply equally to divine cosmogonies and human systems of government. Exploration of physics and meteorology will impinge on a whole range of divine attributes, but it will also affect one's ideas about arbitrary rule on earth. If Zeus looks a little less impressive as a result, so do the tyrant, the king, and the aristocratic 'shepherd of the people'. By removing the wild deuce of superstition from their approach to an argument, the Milesians stimulated free criticism and debate. Once the theology was taken out of causal thinking, it became plain that ideas were, quite simply, competing with one another on their own merits. To operate by the light of reason alone meant abandoning dogma, and with it the whole notion of special privilege in utterance. All now could speak; all must listen.

This advance, we may be certain, bears a more than coincidental relationship to the political evolution that was going on throughout the century. In an undifferentiated society, where all inquiry (*historia*) was regarded as one and indivisible, people would not be slow to apply Milesian methods of thought to the business of ruling the country. It is not until Heracleitus' day, right at the close of the sixth century, that we find a treatise divided up into what became the three traditional sectors of physics, politics and theology: that is, a separate consideration of God, man and nature – Us, Him and That. The gods are not all-pervasive here, even though that handy abstraction 'the divine' (*to theion*) is much in demand as a loophole. True anthropomorphic deities have been relegated to their temples, their god-boxes, and – as in the classic case of Peisistratean Athens – *municipalized*, for the greater glory of the community. Here as elsewhere civic reason has triumphed. What is a free vote in the Assembly but the political analogue of scientific method and inquiry? What is scientific debate but political argument in different terms? The whole pattern of reason hangs together, cognate in every field where it is applied.

One significant by-product of this scientific movement was its direct, and inevitable, impact on religion. We can see this most clearly in Xenophanes of Colophon, who reveals an intellectual's contempt for anthropomorphic tales about the gods (he ridiculed the notion of men envisaging God in their own image), and a *polis*-oriented

124, 125, 126 The Archaic Smile: opposite, head of Apollo, from the Tenea-Volomandra group; top, head of a *kouros* from the Orchomenus-Thera group; above, head of a *kouros* from the Tenea-Volomandra group.

irritation at the immorality, as he saw it, and superstition pervading Homeric epic. Bourgeois respectability is an essentially urban phenomenon, which can often cause severe stress in men's relations with their more eccentric, cruel or sexually indiscriminate tribal deities (Aeschylus' *Prometheus* shows how acute the problem was in Athens a century later). What Xenophanes' monotheistic moralizing reveals is a genuine crisis, not only in the Olympian state religion (which rested on a highly vulnerable basis of anthropomorphizing polytheism), but also in the cult of pure mind – even though it was reason Xenophanes had to thank for the very insights which he achieved. The paradox is classic and perennial. Indeed, the whole sixth-century search for the primal substance – reality and appearance, the One versus the Many – could be seen in religious no less than political terms. What was man's relation to the divine? How were his deep spiritual needs to be fulfilled in a rational age? How were God's ways to be justified to man when man had acquired a new set of municipal ethics, but God disobligingly remained fixed in the old tribal-aristocratic pattern? These were problems which continued to bedevil Greek artists and thinkers throughout the fifth century: Attic drama, to look no further, is full of them. They are still with us today.

127 Mosaic from Baalbek (late third century AD) showing the muse Calliope surrounded by portrait-medallions of Socrates and the Seven Sages – Solon, Thales, Bias of Priene, Cleobulus, Periander, Pittacus of Mytilene, and Chilon. The mosaic is signed 'Amitaios'.

Persia and the West (I): Freedom, autocracy, collaboration

Between 514 and 479 all Greek history is dominated by the gigantic shadow of Persia. The Persian Wars form a logical climax to the whole evolution of Greek society during the sixth century, an integral element in the intellectual revolution of Ionia and the political revolution at Athens. Salamis and Plataea, the great victories of 480 and 479, finally established the right of mainland Greece to pursue its own idiosyncratic way of life without dictatorial pressure from the east. Both Aeschylus and Herodotus concentrated on the theme of freedom versus autocracy, and basically their instinct was sound. After all, a mere handful of Greek states *did* stand out against the whole prevalent trend of Near East palace absolutism; Ionia's thinkers *did* reject the whole theocratic world-view which sustained the Great King; Hellenic strategy *did* outwit the military gigantism of the Persian Empire. It was, indeed, a famous victory.

Yet a simple David-and-Goliath picture (as so often presented) is in many ways seriously misleading. Resistance was limited, by and large, to Athens and the Peloponnesian League, opponents whom Xerxes meant to crush utterly: for them it was a choice between holding out and going under. Most mainland states, on the other hand, saw no good reason to oppose a Persian occupation. Nor did all collaborators side with the invader merely out of fright. Many Greeks, especially in the north, found the prospect of easy-going satrapal rule under the Great King preferable to endless bickering with their own neighbours. In Ionia, rich coastal cities such as Ephesus or Miletus had enjoyed forty prosperous years of Persian overlordship before finally (499) raising the banner of revolt. Canny Sparta stayed neutral till the very last moment: while the Ionians were fighting for Greek freedom, the Spartans took advantage of the situation to crush Argos and reinforce their own position in the Peloponnese. Spartan troops were reluctantly sent to help Athens at the time of the Marathon invasion (490), but got there too late. In 479 it took heavy pressurizing by the Athenians to get a Spartan army north of the Isthmus at all.

Sparta's isolationism was, of course, a special case. Military commitments abroad meant the very real risk of insurrection at home. The Helots, Sparta's downtrodden serf population, were constantly on the brink of revolt. Hence the Spartans' favourite policy during the Persian Wars: build a wall across the Isthmus of Corinth, retreat behind it, and let the rest of Greece go hang. At the same time it must be recognized that not all opponents of direct resistance had such practical motives: many, far from regarding freedom as an unmixed blessing, saw the Persian regime as highly congenial. This is especially true of the Greek aristocracy, who viewed their Iranian counterparts, *en principe*, with a sympathetic eye. For many years now

128 Bust of Herodotus, found at Athritis (modern Benha), Lower Egypt: a Roman copy (probably second century BC) of a late fifth-century Greek original, which can be detected behind several other marble heads – 'a middle-aged man with a high forehead, intelligent, observant eyes, kindly, but not uncritical' (Gisela Richter, *The Portraits of the Greeks*).

in Greece the aristocratic principle of government had come under increasingly heavy fire. This fact not only exaggerated the stubborn conservatism and class prejudice of aristocrats everywhere; it also tended to foster a blood-brotherhood which cut clean across *polis* allegiances, and often even overrode ethnic considerations. The friendship between various Athenian and Spartan noble families, for example, was a fact of capital importance in both cities' history.

Throughout the Aegean world there existed an international and often intermarried network of upper-class elitists, who had far more in common with each other than any of them did with their own democratic governments. Their perennial complaint was that blood no longer counted, that nobodies were everywhere in office, that money and nothing but money dictated contemporary affairs. A considerable body of literature – including the *Odes* of Pindar as well as Theognis' elegiacs and the philosophical fragments of Heracleitus – exemplifies this widespread mood with uncomfortable clarity. It suggests two predictable reactions: on the one hand a retreat into private hedonism, on the other a willingness to collaborate politically with any regime, Greek or foreign, which promised a restoration of the pre-Cleisthenic – or, better, pre-Solonian – *status quo*. Such men turned to Xerxes because they actively preferred the type of government which he offered. Even if they were not power-hungry themselves, they yearned nostalgically for the *ancien régime*.

Thus the Persian Wars became, among other things, a rather subtly deployed class struggle within Greece itself. This is confirmed by one very curious piece of mythologizing which took place – as part of a general conservative reaction – when the wars were over and won. Marathon was at once enshrined as *the* great victory because it had been a land-battle, fought by propertied yeomen in the traditional manner, while Salamis – the true triumph of the Greek genius against odds – was correspondingly depreciated. Naval victories, of course, had, regrettably, to be won by the 'sailor rabble', the lower orders who stank of garlic, bloc-voted at election-time and served as rowers in the fleet. What we have here is violent, almost hysterical, class prejudice on the part of the old elite. Many of the latter, it is true, fought patriotically to stand off Xerxes' war-machine. But they were struggling for the restoration of *their* Greece, the old world of aristocratic privilege, and many of them afterwards must have bitterly regretted their decision.

Some, perhaps the majority, preferred – until confronted with an immediate crisis – to contract out of public affairs altogether, and settle for a life of cultured luxury. Pindar tended to treat the major conflicts of his age (except for an occasional oblique reference) as though they did not exist, and this may have been a commoner upper-

129 Statuette of an athlete binding his hair with a victory fillet (Athens, *c.* 540 BC). The four great athletic festivals, at Olympia, Delphi, Nemea and the Isthmus, attracted competitors and spectators from throughout the Greek world. Victory in any contest was a highly prized honour: famous poets, such as Pindar and Bacchylides, wrote 'Epinician', or Victory Odes for successful athletes, who also received special privileges from their home towns.

class phenomenon than we are accustomed to suppose. 'They bind their hair in golden laurel and take their holiday', Pindar wrote of his Thessalian patrons in 498, while the Ionian Revolt was at its height. A very similar impression is given by contemporary Greek vase-painting. The nearest we come to an acknowledgment of the great conflict between east and west is increased artistic partiality for motifs taken from the *Iliad*. Otherwise the most popular themes remain orgies and drinking-parties (with or without the excuse offered by religious licence). Scenes of leisure and social life abound: significantly, representations of actual work tend to be rare. Pederastic motifs recur with some frequency. The explanation would seem to be that high-quality vase-decoration (whether for export or the home market) catered primarily to upper-class and aristocratic interests, presumably because this group formed the most lucrative market for such wares.

This cultured world of frank sensuality and ever-increasing
naturalism – we find reliefs of dog-fights and hockey, cup-paintings
which depict a vomiting reveller, a courtesan entertaining her balding,
pimply lover – forms a remarkable complement (and one we should
never forget) to the famous public events narrated by Herodotus.
When the time came, it is true, most of Athens' *jeunesse dorée* (like the
Bright Young Things of the 1919–38 era) fought as bravely as anyone;
Marathon revealed a pro-Persian party, but during the next decade

130, 131, 132 Above, left to
right: kylix by the Brygos
Painter (from Vulci, *c.* 490
BC) showing men and women
revelling in the street, probably *en route* from one party to
another (the inner medallion
of this cup shows a vomiting
boy being comforted by a
courtesan); detail of a cup
(kotyle) with homosexual
themes: an old man offering a
cockerel to a youth (fifth century BC); detail of a red-figure
kylix (from Vulci, fifth century BC) showing a male
reveller carrying off a girl.

133, 134 Reliefs from the
'Themistoclean' Wall, in
Athens, used as rubble-fill
during rebuilding (479/8 BC),
but themselves dating back to
c. 510 and 500. Both originally formed part of statue-
bases. Opposite, players bully-
ing-off at hockey; left, two
young men setting a cat to
fight a dog (the latter not
shown here).

resistance stiffened considerably. At Thebes, however, or in Thessaly,
it was quite another matter. Hitherto there had been no such concept
in the Greek-speaking world as ethnic or *polis* treachery; loyalty went,
first and foremost, to the clan. But the Persian Wars demonstrated,
in no uncertain terms, just what order of priorities many Greek
aristocrats respected when it came to the crunch. It was those fateful
years that produced the term 'Medism': at first, treacherous commerce
with the Persians, then, by extension, collaboration of any sort.

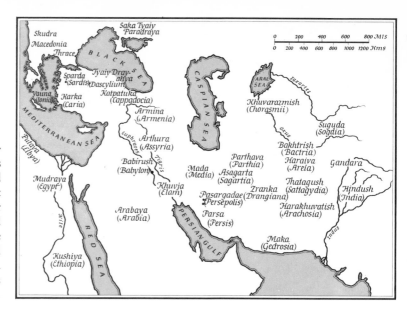

135 Map of the Persian satrapies: Greek transliterations of Persian names are listed second, in brackets. The exact frontiers remain a matter for speculation. The Empire had already existed under the Medes ('satrapy' seems derived from a Median rather than a Persian word) but reached its greatest extent under Darius I.

The map contains the following labels:

Skudra · Macedonia · Thrace · BLACK SEA · Saka Tyaiy Paradraya · ARAL SEA · Jaxartes · Sparda (Sardis) · Tyaiy Drayahya · Dascylium · Yauna (Ionia) · Karka (Caria) · Katpatuka (Cappadocia) · Khuvarazmish (Chorasmii) · Suguda (Sogdia) · MEDITERRANEAN SEA · Putaya (Libya) · Euphrates · Armina (Armenia) · CASPIAN SEA · Oxus · Bakhtrish (Bactria) · Haraiva (Areia) · Gandara · Arthura (Assyria) · Babirush (Babylon) · Tigris · Mada (Media) · Parthava (Parthia) · Asagarta (Sagartia) · Thatagush (Sattagydia) · Hindush (India) · Mudraya (Egypt) · Khuvja (Elam) · Pasargadae (Drangiana) · Persepolis · Zranka (Drangiana) · Harakhuvatish (Arachosia) · Arabaya (Arabia) · Parsa (Persis) · PERSIAN GULF · Maka (Gedrosia) · Indus · Nile · RED SEA · Kushiya (Ethiopia)

Persia and the West (II): Hellenism triumphant

By 500, perhaps earlier, Persia's growing interest in Europe was unmistakable. From Darius' first invasion of Thrace (and the subsequent establishment of Persian control over the Hellespont and Bosporus) to his recognition of Hippias the Peisistratid, the writing on the wall became increasingly clear. The Ionian Revolt was, in one sense, an attempt to stave off the inevitable by taking the initiative and counter-attacking at source. Its final collapse (494) made a Persian invasion of the mainland almost inevitable. Apart from anything else, prestige was involved. An Athenian contingent had, c. 498, burnt down Sardis, the capital of Lydia and a satrapal seat. Darius did not take the affront lightly. In 492 he sent out an expedition under his son-in-law Mardonius to teach these presumptuous Greeks a sharp lesson. Mardonius' fleet was wrecked in a storm off the Athos peninsula, and he himself wounded during a brush with Thracian tribesmen. Greece had obtained a brief respite; but it was clear, now, what the final outcome must be.

In 491 Darius tested the morale of the Greek states by sending round envoys demanding earth and water in token of vassalage. At Athens and Sparta they were roughly handled. But – more important – all the islands and many mainland cities submitted without protest. Darius decided the omens were good. The next year (490) he sent another fleet across the Aegean, with Athens as its specific target. Old Hippias accompanied the expedition: a doddering but inevitable choice as head of any Persian-backed Athenian government, and encouraged by assurances from Peisistratid supporters within the

136 Detail from the south portico bas-relief of the Treasury of Darius at Persepolis (sixth–fifth century BC), showing Darius I (r. 521–486 BC) sitting in state.

137 Above: inscribed herm (from Ravenna) of Miltiades, son of Cimon, former ruler of the Thracian Chersonese, and victor of Marathon (*c.* 550–489 BC).

138 Above right: aerial view of the Marathon plain, scene of the battle between the Greeks and Persians, 490 BC.

139 Right: Corinthian bronze helmet (Olympia, *c.* 490 BC) inscribed 'Miltiades dedicated me', and in all likelihood that which he wore during the battle.

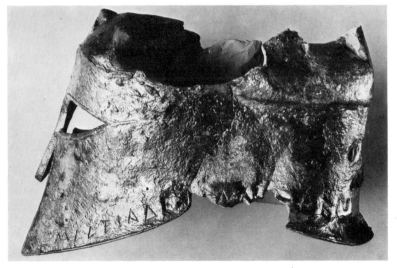

walls. The Persians landed at Marathon beach, just as Peisistratus had done at the time of his final bid for power (546). The plain was well suited to cavalry. In Athens it was decided to 'take rations and march'. Nine thousand Athenian hoplites, aided by a thousand Plataeans, defeated this Persian task-force in a brilliantly executed battle for which chief credit must go to Miltiades. The Persians sailed home, and Athens breathed again.

It had, indeed, been a famous victory; but it offered no sort of final solution, merely gave mainland Greece a breathing-space to prepare against the major invasion which was bound to follow. As a boost to Athenian morale, on the other hand, it was of incalculable value – not least by demonstrating that Greek hoplites could defeat a Persian army *on land*, something the Ionians had never contrived to do. The legend, indeed, became more important than the actual battle: the 'men of Marathon' came to be identified with every old-fashioned conservative

140 Piece of red-figure Attic bowl by Douris (fifth century BC), showing an Athenian standing triumphant over a prostrate Persian.

virtue. Yet Marathon in fact marked the end of the old regime. From now on, increasingly, Athens' future as a major Aegean power lay, not with aristocratic cavalrymen or yeomen-hoplites, but with the despised 'sailor rabble' that manned the triremes. The architect of this new-style navy, Themistocles, stands at the very centre of Athenian history during the crucial years between 493 (when he was elected archon) and 479, when, his task accomplished, he found himself rapidly eased out of effective power by the conservative opposition.

Most Athenians were convinced that 'the Persian defeat at Marathon meant the end of the war'. Themistocles knew better: this cannot have made him popular, especially with the landed tories, who gave Marathon almost mystical significance. If Athens was to be defended against a full-scale invasion, he reasoned, several ends must be achieved. Somehow the Assembly must be brought to back a naval development programme: Themistocles was already certain in his own mind that only at sea, or through amphibious operations, could Greece stand off the Persian war-machine. This meant effectively neutralizing the aristocratic conservatives, whose credo called for a land-based defence scheme. It also meant finding some formula for continuity of government, since planning against Persia was essentially a long-term operation. Lastly, to implement this programme meant finding a reliable and extensive source of capital. In the years between Marathon and Salamis solutions were found to all these problems: once again, it is Themistocles who must get the lion's share of the credit.

To eliminate the opposition called for some tough political in-fighting. Miltiades, the old-guard victor of Marathon, was prosecuted after an unsuccessful campaign against Paros (489), and died in prison of gangrene. Themistocles also found, in the Cleisthenic statute-book, a hitherto unused device known as 'ostracism'. A quorum of six thousand votes by the citizen body could send any person into political exile for ten years, without loss of property or civil rights, on the grounds that his temporary removal would benefit the *polis* as a whole. The system got its name from the potsherds (*ostraka*) on which the candidates' names were scratched: many of these have been found during excavations in the Agora and elsewhere. By skilful manipula-tion of this device Themistocles and his supporters got rid of several leading reactionaries – and, more important, potential collaborators with Persia.

Governmental continuity called for different tactics. The archon-ship, as Themistocles knew to his cost, was a thoroughly wasteful institution, since no man could hold it more than once, for twelve months only. The Areopagus Council hardly had a grip on day-to-day affairs. Two things had to be done here. First, find an appropriate

office which could be held, legitimately, year after year. Second, change the conditions of the archonship in such a way that it no longer attracted first-class men. The office was found in the recently instituted ten tribal *strategoi*, or Board of Generals, who – military competence being something better not left to chance – could be re-elected annually. To depreciate the archonship, Themistocles simply got a motion passed (487) that henceforth appointment to it should be by sortition, or lot. The result, of course, was that ambitious men tended more and more to canvass for the Board of Generals, while the archonship went increasingly to nonentities. Since the Areopagus Council was recruited exclusively from ex-archons, it too in course of time became fatally weakened.

There remained two key problems: finance and naval rearmament. At first it looked as though both might fail of solution. Luckily, Athens got a few years' grace at this crucial point: rebellion in Egypt, followed by the death of Darius (November 486), kept Persia busy for a while. Soon, however, alarming reports began to come in that Xerxes, Darius' successor, was building a major invasion fleet. Then, with impeccable timing, a rich and seemingly inexhaustible new vein of silver was struck in the Athenian mines at Laurium, near Cape Sunium. The state's surplus that year amounted to no less than one hundred talents, and argument raged in the Assembly as to how this increase of capital should be applied. The conservatives, led by

141 Above left: section of the 'Themistoclean' city wall, west of the Sacred Gate. The repairs above the main ashlar blocks were carried out in the fourth century BC by Conon and Demosthenes.

142 Above: bust of Themistocles (Roman Antonine copy of a Greek original perhaps to be dated *c.* 460 BC). Despite much argument, it is now generally agreed that this 'Ostia herm' can be accepted as a genuine, if formalized, portrait of Themistocles, perhaps as he was during his Persian exile, while Governor of Magnesia. The heavy, pugnacious, humorous features shown here do nothing to contradict this assumption.

143 East Gate of the Tri-
pylon, Persepolis (sixth–fifth
century BC) showing relief of
Darius   enthroned,   with
Xerxes, his Crown Prince, in
attendance.

144 Remains of the ship-sheds, Zea Harbour, Piraeus.

Aristeides, known as 'the Just', wanted a general hand-out to those on the citizen-roll, at ten drachmas a head. Themistocles' naval group, predictably, demanded a fleet. Deadlock led to yet another ostracism (482); Aristeides went into exile, and at the eleventh hour a crash programme of shipbuilding, at the rate of a hundred triremes per annum, got under way in the half-finished Piraeus yards.

It was none too soon. In spring 481 Xerxes' vast amphibious host set out from Asia. Alarming propaganda, some of it perhaps even true, reached Greece: Persian troops and baggage-animals were said to be so numerous that they drank the rivers dry. The Delphic Oracle, understandably, was pessimistic about Athens' chances, but under pressure came up with an ambiguous prophecy concerning Salamis and Athens' 'wooden walls'. Fleet or Acropolis? Opinions were divided. An attempt by the Greeks to hold Tempe in northern Greece proved a fiasco, and Themistocles, at last, got his chance. A famous motion was passed in the Athenian Assembly (against shocked conservative opposition) to evacuate Athens, and 'to meet the enemy at Artemisium in Euboea', while a Spartan-led force held Thermo-pylae, the narrow coastal pass on the mainland opposite. For several days it looked as though this strategy might succeed. King Leonidas and his Spartans stood off every Persian assault, while the Greek fleet got the better of the Persians by sea, and an opportune storm wrecked many more of their vessels on a lee shore. Then a local guide, Ephialtes, showed Xerxes a mountain path by which Leonidas' position could be turned. The Spartans at Thermopylae went down fighting, Artemisium was abandoned, and the road to the south lay open.

145 Below: bronze figurine of cloaked and helmeted warrior: early fifth century BC, probably Spartan. Note the tresses lying neatly over his shoulders – reminding us that at Thermopylae, before the battle, 'the Spartans on the sea-wet rock sat down and combed their hair' (A. E. Housman).

146 Right: marble statue of a warrior sometimes identified as Leonidas (Laconia, 490–480 BC).

147 Above: the Gyphtokas-tro Pass over Cithaeron, show-ing the fort now known as Gyphtokastro, generally iden-tified with the ancient Eleu-therae.

148 Left: detail of the 'serpent-column' erected at Delphi by the Greek states as a memorial of the Persian Wars. The original bore the name of Pausanias the Spartan regent; the Spartans erased it and sub-stituted the names of thirty-one cities, with the inscription 'These fought in the war'. Originally the three twining serpents supported a gold tri-pod on their heads. What sur-vives is now in the Hippo-drome at Constantinople (Istanbul).

Themistocles pulled out his battered squadrons, completed the evacuation of Athens, and, with his Spartan fellow commander, set up a new allied headquarters on the nearby island of Salamis. The strategy by which he lured a large Persian fleet into the Salamis narrows, and there annihilated it in a most brilliant naval battle, is vividly described by both Herodotus and Aeschylus. The latter's eyewitness account offers a particularly valuable 'rowing-bench view' of the action and subsequent rout. As he makes his Persian messenger report:

> Crushed hulls lay upturned on the sea, so thick
> You could not see the water, choked with wrecks
> And slaughtered men; while all the shores and reefs
> Were strewn with corpses . . .

Xerxes at once pulled out and marched home to Susa, leaving Mardonius behind with a streamlined professional army of perhaps thirty thousand men. Next year (479) an allied Greek task-force under Pausanias, Regent of Sparta and Captain-General of the Hellenes, brought Mardonius to battle at Plataea in Boeotia. At the same time a final naval battle was fought off Mycale, in the eastern Aegean. Both were overwhelming Greek victories. Now, at last, the shadow of Persian invasion was lifted from the mainland, and a new era in Greek history began.

149 A seal impression depicting a trireme, found at Persepolis, and probably dating to the reign of Xerxes (485–465 BC). Triremes are known to have been the chief vessels in the fleet of Xerxes.

4

Democracy and empire:
the paradigm of Athens
(478–404 BC)

The growth of Athenian imperialism

The Persian Wars created, at Athens in particular, a temporary upsurge of *polis* patriotism overriding faction or class. This trend is well symbolized by. a story told of young Cimon, Miltiades' son. Before Salamis he led a procession of upper-class youths to Athena's shrine on the Acropolis, where they all solemnly dedicated their bridles, symbol of the cavalry class. This done, they applied for seats on the rowing-benches of the new triremes – a striking acknowledgment of the fact that, for the duration at least, the navy had first claim on Athens' defenders. But the fundamental split in Athenian society – between Cleisthenes' new voters, and the upper classes looking back to some romanticized 'ancestral constitution' – was only papered over by the common emergency of Xerxes' invasion. From now on it became a permanent, and highly abrasive, feature of the city's political life, often with disastrous consequences. Two decades of aristocratic-conservative rule were followed by a swing to democratic progressivism (both terms are approximate only) which, with brief intervals, lasted throughout the rest of the fifth century.

In 479/8 Athens had not only a large and effective fleet, but also a first-class new harbour, now nearing completion, in Piraeus. This suggested one obvious alternative to Sparta's land-based Peloponnesian League: an independent maritime federation, to which member-states would contribute either ships or cash, its ostensible purpose an offensive-defensive alliance against Persia. Such a body, known as the 'Delian League' because it had its treasury on Delos, under Apollo's protection, was formed as early as 478/7, in a breakaway movement from the general 'Hellenic League' which had fought the campaign against Xerxes. Aristeides the Just was given the

150 Reverse of an Athenian silver tetradrachm (*c.* 480–460 BC) showing Athena's sacred owl, the little *glaux*, with a spray of the goddess's olive, and the Greek letters ATHE (nai).

151 Detail of amphora, fifth century BC, showing an old man of the leisured class followed by a small Negro slave.

unenviable task of assessing members' contributions. From this moment Athens and the Peloponnesian bloc became, inevitably, political (and to some extent commercial) rivals in the Aegean. Furthermore, the Delian League contained the seeds of Athenian imperialism in it *ab initio*. All but the biggest and strongest maritime states – Lesbos, Samos, Chios – would, sooner rather than later, find it easier to supply tribute rather than ships, thus leaving Athens with the whip-hand in terms of effective power.

So, indeed, it turned out. The first attempted secession from the League came only eight or nine years after its inception, when the island of Naxos rebelled (470/69), was besieged, and bullied into submission. No one protested. From then on, as Thucydides for one sees very clearly, there could be no doubt how Athens – whether conservatives or progressives were in power – would treat her so-called 'allies' when it came to a show-down. Member-states did, it is true, enjoy certain benefits from Athenian rule, chief among them

being efficient policing of the seas, and protection against external interference. But the price was a heavy one, and paid not only in cash. As time went on, a series of increasingly stringent regulations, covering everything from weights and measures to compulsory religious observances, made it clear that League members had lost their real autonomy, were subjects rather than allies. Numerous rebellions strongly suggest an ingrained reluctance to embrace efficiency at the expense of freedom. Independence, however chaotic, was all.

It is surprising how fast, once peace had been won, public opinion swung back to aristocratic traditionalism in Athens. Until about 462 the conservative faction enjoyed a remarkable resurgence of power. The hero of the 470s was no longer Themistocles, but Miltiades' dashing, handsome, wealthy son Cimon: an ideal reactionary figurehead. Despite Salamis, the 'sailor rabble' were not, to many people's satisfaction, getting things their own way. Cimon went from strength

152 Detail of cup with medallion portraying an Athenian horseman, probably of the cavalry class, by Onesimos, c. 475 BC.

153 Metal weight in the form of an astragal, weighing 930 gm, from Gela, Sicily.

to strength. He captured Eion, a valuable port on the Strymon. He brought home what were reputed to be the bones of Theseus from Scyros. He built public squares in Athens, extended the southern bastion of the Acropolis, threw his gardens open to the public and basked in a haze of benevolent aristocratic patronage. Meanwhile, conservative opinion at Athens and Sparta alike (most probably in collusion) was working against the two maverick architects of victory in the Persian Wars. Themistocles finally found himself ostracized (471) on a charge – supreme irony – of collaborating with the Persians. He spent the next five or six years in Argos, plotting against Sparta. Pausanias came under suspicion of inciting the Helots to revolt, and in 466 was arrested and starved to death. At the same time the democracy in Argos was ousted by a right-wing coup, and Themistocles (hearing he was to be tried for Medism *in absentia*, and

guessing the verdict in advance) wisely fled the country. Paradox on paradox: in 465, finding all other paths barred to him, he actually reached Persian territory as a suppliant – and very soon found himself established as the Great King's Governor of Magnesia.

Probably in 469, Cimon took a large fleet to the eastern Mediterranean and routed Persia's forces by land and sea at the Battle of the Eurymedon River. This not only brought home a great mass of booty, but reopened the old Levant trade-route to Rhodes, Cyprus, Phoenicia and Egypt. Athenian vessels now enjoyed the general freedom of the seas, and the conservatives' position in Athens must have seemed unassailable. Next year, at the apogee of his power, Cimon and his fellow commanders acted as judges at the Greater Dionysia, an unprecedented special privilege. They chose a young, but safely conservative, playwright called Sophocles against the older,

154 The Theatre of Dionysus seen from the Acropolis, looking south. These remains do not predate the fourth century BC, though dramatic and musical contests had been shifted to this site from the Agora at least as early as the 440s. A simple stone theatre was then erected, but only a few blocks survive, assimilated to the later edifice associated with the name of Lycurgus.

155 Bust of Aeschylus, from the Farnese Collection. Portraits seem to have been rare in antiquity, and no surviving likeness can be securely ascribed. The legend that Aeschylus' death was caused by an eagle dropping a tortoise on his head to crack it open (having mistaken the poet's head for a stone) can hardly be taken as evidence of baldness.

more famous, but (as they saw it) dangerously radical Aeschylus, thus providing the first – but by no means the last – known instance in history of a literary prize being awarded for non-literary, *i.e.* political, reasons.

Cimon and his aristocratic friends were, in fact, less secure than might appear on the surface. A new generation of intellectual populists, led by Ephialtes and the young Pericles, now began to make itself felt in home affairs. A major attack was launched against the privileges of the Areopagus Council, still seen as the very symbol and bulwark of conservatism. In 464, when a serious earthquake at Sparta was followed by a Helot revolt, Cimon urged the Assembly to send help to the Spartans. A force was duly sent, under Cimon himself, but proved so unpredictable in its sympathies that the Spartan authorities soon sent such dangerous allies home again, in case they ended up fighting on the wrong side. The blow to Cimon's prestige was enormous; nor did he improve matters by a tooth-and-nail opposition to Ephialtes' anti-Areopagite legislation. Too stupid to know when the political tide had turned against him, he went down fighting, and in 461 found himself ostracized. The reforms went through that same year; shortly afterwards Ephialtes was assassinated by some disgruntled reactionaries who tried to pin the murder on Pericles. This can be seen as a last angry gesture of despair: the radicals were now firmly in power, and there, by and large, they stayed.

During the next twelve years Athens embarked on a policy of calculated imperial aggression which bears Pericles' unmistakable hallmark. With a steadily rising population, the problem of importing adequate grain supplies – Attica had long ceased to be self-supporting – now acquired top priority. Support offered at the right moment (460/59) to a native pretender in Egypt gave Athens a guaranteed granary for the next six years. Egypt was lost to Persia, and the only real Greek casualty in this episode was Themistocles, who chose honourable suicide rather than take the field at the Great King's bidding against his fellow countrymen. The extent of Athenian military commitments during this period can be gauged from a 459 casualty-list, containing the names of those who died that year in Cyprus, Egypt, Halieis, Aegina and the Megarid. A Corinthian attack was beaten off (458), and that same year Athens began the construction of her Long Walls between the city and Piraeus. In 457 she forced Aegina's surrender, and won a resounding victory at Oenophyta, which left all Boeotia apart from Thebes part of an Athenian land-empire. Yet within a few years the whole imposing edifice had collapsed. Why?

Probably in 455 the Messenian-Helot stronghold of Ithome at last fell to Sparta, thus releasing her formidable army for action elsewhere.

The following year a Persian general annihilated the Athenian fleet and garrison in Egypt, so that Athens at one stroke lost her guaranteed source of grain. Also in 454, by no coincidence, the Athenian League's treasury was transferred from Delos to Athens (where no allied check could be kept on it) and a new wave of revolts broke out among the subject-allies. In 451/0 Athens suffered a famine, and that same spring a five-year truce was negotiated with the Peloponnesian League. Cash reserves might be high, but silver remained inedible. Cimon, back from exile, tried to recoup matters in Cyprus and Egypt, but died at the outset of his campaign (450). Faced with this crisis, Athens had no option but to negotiate with Persia. The Peace of Callias (449) formally terminated hostilities between the two powers – thereby proclaiming the Delian League a dead letter. Time, however, was more valuable to Pericles at this moment than the subject-allies' approval. Famine had barely been averted, the Spartans precariously stalled. The empire was now placated by a full year's remission of tribute (448/7). It had been a close call, but Athens survived – to embark, under a new Periclean policy, on the most glorious decades of her entire history.

156 Marble herm of Pericles, found at Tivoli: Roman copy of an original (?) by Cresilas (c. 430 BC). Since Pericles suffered from a slightly deformed elongation of the skull (unkind comic poets described him as 'squill-headed'), most artists chose to portray him wearing a helmet. Ironically, he was said to be the near-double of Peisistratus – an accident of which his political enemies took full advantage.

The Periclean ascendency

The history of the years 449 to 431 is a strange and in some ways paradoxical amalgam: of power politics and great architecture, sculpture and sophistry, creative ferment and reactionary legislation, economic crisis and civic overspending, radical ideals and imperialist authoritarianism. Across the brilliance of those two hectic decades in Athens there steadily lengthens the dark shadow of imminent and inevitable war. Over the whole scene – like that Olympian Zeus to whom he was so often, and by no means as a compliment, compared – there broods the enigmatic presence of the epoch's guiding spirit, Pericles. A ruthless but by no means infallible power-politician, Pericles had a vision of Athenian greatness indeed, though one less exclusively based on cultural uplift than modern Hellenophiles often like to believe. What he wanted for his city was, in the last resort, simply the Peisistratean formula on a bigger and better scale than ever before – more splendid (and splendidly ostentatious) public buildings, a sounder economy geared to imperial tribute, and a determination to justify Athens' leading role in Aegean affairs through moral superiority as well as an unbeatable fleet. Athens was to be the 'educator of Hellas'; if any excuse were needed for her political expansionism, this phrase provided it.

Let us sketch the events of those crowded eighteen years, and watch Pericles at work. The tone is set immediately after the Peace of Callias, when the whole *raison d'être* of an Athenian-led 'defence league' had collapsed, and her allies were understandably restive. Now during the Persian Wars the Greek allies had sworn a solemn oath which bound them, *inter alia*, to leave all burnt temples in ruins, as a memorial of Persian vandalism. This oath had been kept with, to us, surprising fidelity, and constituted a major obstacle for those who nursed Peisistratean ambitions in the field of civic development. However, the conclusion of peace with Persia was held to render the oath void. It was against this background that, in 449, Pericles proposed an inter-state Panhellenic Congress, to be held at Athens, with three main items on the agenda: restoration of shrines destroyed by the Persians, establishment of the sacrifices vowed to the gods in 480, and the policing of the seas.

Sparta at once vetoed such a conference: to have accepted would have been tantamount to acknowledging Athens' supremacy in the Aegean. Pericles may well have foreseen such a reaction, and welcomed it. What he had to get was a public excuse for unilateral action: this the boycott provided. Coolly arguing that Athens had suffered more war damage than any other city during the Persian invasions, he now earmarked five thousand talents from accumulated allied funds for the restoration of Athens' own sacred buildings, thus solving the question

157 View of the Parthenon from the west-north-west, just inside the Propylaea. This splendid Doric temple, of fine Pentelic marble, has become the very symbol, not only of Periclean Athens, but of the 'classical spirit', something more often invoked than defined.

158 The Propylaea, from the west front of the Parthenon: the great marble ramp lies directly behind the columned fivefold gateway. To the right, the north wing, known in antiquity as the Pinakotheke, or 'picture-gallery'.

159 The little Temple of Athena Nike ('Victory'). It was built in the Ionic order, with four columns at either end of a simple cella, by Callicrates (c. 427–425 BC), pulled down in 1687 to make way for a gun-emplacement, and twice reconstructed (1835–36, 1935–40).

160 View of the Erechtheum from the Parthenon, looking towards the north face of the Acropolis: from left to right, the Porch of the Caryatids, the south wall of the cella, and the East Porch. Its odd architectural plan was due to the various archaic shrines which had to be incorporated in or round it. Begun in 421 BC to commemorate the Peace of Nicias; completed (after at least two breaks) in 407/6. The site is that of Athens' Mycenaean palace.

161–3 Three details from the Panathenaic frieze of the Parthenon, of Parian marble, finally completed, together with the metopes and pedimental sculptures, by 432 BC. Right: a sacrificial heifer being led in the Panathenaic procession (south frieze); below, horsemen riding to join the procession (west frieze); below right, a youth leading horses (west frieze).

of what to do with the League's cash surplus now peace had been made. He could, as A. French says, plausibly argue that this money represented a 'proper offset to war damage suffered by members', and was now – in default of an official Congress to vote on the matter – being applied for just that purpose. At all events, the stage was now set for that great civic building programme on which so much of Pericles' fame rests, its most notable items being the Parthenon and the Propylaea.

The precise motives for embarking on so costly a programme at this point have never been satisfactorily determined. Piety of the conventional sort played little part in the scheme: the Parthenon had nothing to do with the numinous cult of Athena Polias and her age-old olive-wood totem (*xoanon*) on the north side of the Acropolis, while the Propylaea was a wholly secular construction. It is worth noting that after Pericles' death, this programme was permanently abandoned (the Propylaea being left incomplete, as it stood at the outbreak of war) and replaced by projects of a more modest and traditionally religious sort: the Erechtheum, the exquisite little Temple of Athena Nike. The Parthenon was essentially a monument to civic pride. Yet civic pride is not, in itself, a wholly sufficient explanation. Plutarch suggests (perhaps on the basis of opposition propaganda) that one aim which Pericles had in mind was to mop up a solid core of domestic unemployment by floating long-term public works schemes – always a popular standby with rulers jittery about the urban mob. The regular *cleruchies* (*i.e.* colonies of Athenian citizens) sent out during this period do suggest a surplus population of potential trouble-makers, as well as the need to establish garrison outposts in the Aegean.

One year's remission of tribute was a time-winning gesture in a crisis, but nothing more. There followed a general tightening-up of central control on Athens' part over what was henceforth, beyond any doubt, an empire in the full sense. Increasingly harsh taxation, with local Athenian inspectors to enforce prompt payment, was accompanied by somewhat *recherché* civic-cum-religious requirements (the Peisistratean touch again): the allies, for instance, were obliged to bring a sacrificial cow and a panoply, or full suit of armour, to the annual festival of the Greater Dionysia. In 447 the imperial administration was still shaky after its great crisis, as we can see from that year's tribute-list, notable for part-payments and defaulting absentees. But by 446 control was well established once more – and not before time. Boeotia had been lost at the disastrous Battle of Coronea (447/6), and Athens' land-empire melted away overnight. The expiry of her five-year truce with the Peloponnesian League a few months afterwards was followed by a Spartan invasion. This immediate danger Pericles averted with a well-placed bribe (the attacking force turned back home at Eleusis), and he then signed a somewhat disadvantageous peace treaty.

Both sides were left with their relative spheres of power more or less intact. The treaty endorsed that *de facto* Athens–Sparta dualism – each city backed by its cluster of hard–core allies – which made the Peloponnesian War an ultimate inevitability. It also, however, deprived Athens (by requiring her to cede Megara's ports, Pagae and Nisaea) of an alternative Isthmus crossing to that provided by Corinth, and hence of a secure trade–route to the west. Western imports, of grain and timber in particular, were becoming increasingly vital to Athens as time went on: no accident that in the year after the peace treaty (445) yet another famine hit the city, and was only met by a stop–gap consignment of wheat from an Egyptian pretender in the Delta. Sooner or later, it was clear, Megara would have to be cajoled or coerced into rejoining Athens, an alternative Isthmus crossing be made good (at present Athenian traffic was dependent on Corinth's good will), and a firm foothold established in Sicily or Magna Graecia (southern Italy), as well as at key–points all along the route. Much of Periclean foreign

164 Model of the forty foot gold and ivory (chryselephantine) statue of Athena Parthenos, seen here against the rear wall of the cella.

policy in the years that followed was directed towards these ends.

The 'Olympian' and his friends did not have things all their own way at home: it would be a serious mistake to suppose Pericles the object of universal veneration among his contemporaries. The comic playwrights abused him with lethal scurrility (and what comes across as real and undisguised loathing) for his moral superiority and icy self-esteem. The conservative opposition, now led by Thucydides, son of Melesias (perhaps the historian's great-uncle), lambasted his building programme and his waste of public revenues, comparing the new Athens to a bedizened whore, 'with her jewels and her images and her thousand-talent temples' – the latter a fair charge if we add in the cost of the great chryselephantine statue of Athena designed by Pericles' friend Pheidias. In 443, however, Thucydides was ostracized, a move which temporarily broke the back of the opposition, and Pericles entered on the first of fifteen unbroken terms as *strategos* (general) – which meant, as critics lost no time in pointing out, that he was not obliged to submit his accounts for scrutiny in the new year. One of the first things he and his colleagues now did was to overhaul

165 Portrait-head identified (on rather flimsy grounds) as Pheidias, the sculptor, painter and engraver (?copy of likeness *c.* 300 BC). A bald old man wielding a battle-axe or a rock appears in copies of the shield of Pheidias' Athena Parthenos: Plutarch tells us that Pheidias put himself in the Battle of Greeks and Amazons in just such a pose.

166 Below: base of an Athenian black cup found in Pheidias' workshop at Olympia (together with terracotta moulds for the gold draperies of his giant statue of Zeus), and inscribed with the graffito 'I am Pheidias's'.

the financial system, on a regional basis: for so lofty an intellectual Pericles had a highly practical streak over money matters. One of the financial officers he appointed – an equally characteristic touch – was Sophocles the dramatist.

Throughout this decade, not surprisingly, Sophocles found himself preoccupied with a crucial theme, one central to the fundamentally civic and secular world of Periclean *polis* government, with its underlying intellectual rationalism. Himself a religious traditionalist by temperament, he saw that the 'ancestral ways', appealing to a man's instincts and emotions more deeply than any mere ethical or rational allegiance, had much right and psychological weight on their side. How to reconcile them with the centralized justice and nascent bourgeois morality of the new Athens? How to integrate kinship and bureaucracy, the claims of clan and state? When the two codes clashed, as they were bound to do, where was the individual to stand on a moral issue? Both in the *Ajax* (?446) and the *Antigone* (442) Sophocles takes what strikes us as the grotesque problem of burial-rights, and through it shows how the clash between *polis* and family could land the uncompromising man (or woman) of principle in an insoluble dilemma. The trouble with Antigone and Creon is that they simply

167 Detail of a Lucanian nestoris by the Dolon Painter (*c.* 380–370 BC): scene from Sophocles' *Antigone*, showing Antigone brought before Creon by two guards.

lack common grounds for discussion. This polarization of attitudes ended by colouring the entire fabric of fifth-century Athens.

Meanwhile Pericles, with clear foresight, saw war coming up like a storm-cloud out of the Peloponnese, and made careful preparations to face it. Financial reserves had never stood higher. The treasures of Attica's rural temples and the lower city were transferred, as a safety measure, to the Acropolis. A stringent trade embargo was imposed on Megara (autumn 433). As the crisis mounted, another attempt was made to get at Pericles by prosecuting his friends (Pheidias and the Olympian's mistress Aspasia had earlier suffered from similar attacks). In 432 a decree was passed providing for stringent penalties against atheism, and clearly aimed at the freethinking philosopher Anaxagoras, who left town in a hurry. Constant embassies from Sparta and Corinth tried to make Pericles compromise, at least over Megara, but without success. The revolt of Potidaea in Chalcidice merely sharpened his resolution. So, in spring 431, Athenian Empire and Peloponnesian League finally went to war. Their struggle lasted, with uneasy intervals, for twenty-seven years, destroyed Periclean Athens, and might have been largely forgotten except for a sick and bitter historian who fought in the war himself, intuitively grasped its importance, and wrote an account of it which has remained – as he planned that it should – a 'possession for all time'.

168 Portrait of Thucydides the historian: copy of an (?) early fourth-century BC original. Other busts, clearly based on the same original, suggest that we may have here a genuine likeness, perhaps executed after Thucydides' recall to Athens in 404/3 BC, or at the time of his death a few years later.

Sophists, scientists, witch-hunters

The social unrest engendered by a steadily widening dissemination of intellectual notions concerning the nature of matter, and (perhaps more important) of the heavens, becomes unmistakable as the fifth century wears on. The whole drift of the New Learning – not in speculative fields alone, but in related disciplines such as medicine or forensic oratory – was towards a firmly hominocentric rationalism. In Xenophanes' day the gods had been criticized: that was because they still mattered to thinking people. Now they were simply being left out of an intellectual's calculations – or, worse, replaced by fringe-benefit mysticism: exotic, enthusiastic, and decidedly uncivic foreign cults. The emphasis laid by Athens on the Eleusinian Mysteries represented an attempt to provide this potentially anarchic trend with some official outlook. Its logical outcome would be, later, the vague, blissful, remote and irrelevant gods of Epicurus or Lucretius: a mere calculated genuflection to traditional beliefs, while the real business of the intellectual world was being analysed elsewhere.

The most significant fifth-century manifestation of this movement can be seen in Euripides, whose anti-clericalism borrowed the smooth in-fighting techniques perfected by Athens' political orators. His formula was simple, and left him proof against prosecution by any

outraged pious conservative. He would first ransack all available sources (he was a very bookish man) for the most archaic and disreputable myths in the tradition, anything which showed up the gods in a bad light by contemporary standards of civic morality (his treatment of Apollo in the *Ion* is a good example). He would then write a play round this theme in strictly human, and most often domestic, terms, with the kind of social and psychological realism most calculated to annoy traditionalists. Having done all this, he would, at the very last moment, as a kind of carefully planned insult, produce some god or goddess – the *deus* literally *ex machina* – to pick up the pieces, sort out the characters' moral destinies, marry them off to each other and produce a few stunning platitudes by way of coda.

This whole state of affairs constituted a cumulative assault on what Gilbert Murray, in a striking geological metaphor, once called the 'inherited conglomerate' of socio-religious belief. The young smelt something exciting in the air. The old became uneasy and alarmed: what reached *their* noses was the cold stench of atheism. Unlike Parmenides the philosopher, they trusted their own senses, and were uneasily aware of something rotten in the state. The progressive freethinkers who formed Pericles' private circle, Anaxagoras in particular, presented an obvious and tempting target for their resentment. The originality and subtlety of Anaxagoras' notion of Mind as the moving force in the universe would be lost on them. What *they* could see were his secularism, his lack of interest in public affairs, his disrespect for the gods, his embarrassing theories about the heavenly bodies. Euripides not only quoted such views with zest and approval – in one fragment he refers to the sun as a 'golden clod' – but had himself read the Milesian philosophers, and peddled their unorthodoxies whenever he got the chance.

169, 170, 171 Opposite, far left: the Grotto of Hades at Eleusis, where Persephone is said to have been restored to earth from the underworld. Left: detail of marble relief (second half of fifth century BC) from Eleusis, eleven miles west of Athens, the great centre of Demeter's cult and of the Eleusinian Mysteries. Kore (Persephone), daughter of Demeter, places a crown on the head of Triptolemus, while on his left (not shown here) Demeter herself offers him an ear of grain. Below: bridge on the Sacred Way, just outside the Dipylon Gate, between Athens and Eleusis.

172 Below: relief showing Euripides, seated, being presented with a tragic mask by a female personification of 'The Stage' (*Skene*), who has a scroll in her right hand, while Dionysus, patron deity of drama, looks on, holding a wine-cup (*kantharos*).

173 Marble herm of Plato (possibly copied from an original by Silanion), and for long a disappointment to the philosopher's more romantic admirers: 'Could this crosslooking individual be the idealistic, mystical, poetical Plato?' they wondered (Richter, *Portraits of the Greeks*). It could be; it was. Indeed, the wide forehead, the brooding and aristocratic expression, correspond well with other descriptions of Plato known from antiquity.

The main disseminators of the New Learning, however, were a group of men – mostly non-Athenians – known as 'Sophists', a term which implies the teaching of technical skills. These itinerant professors undoubtedly filled an educational gap; they also shocked traditionalists by taking fat fees in return for their services. Among modern scholars their reputation has varied. Plato's picture of immoral and radical logic-choppers corrupting the young for cash was severely dented by the rise of modern totalitarianism, which at once made Plato himself look uncommonly like a proto-fascist, and therefore automatically suspect as a witness. The Sophists were then revamped as pioneers of the great liberal movement. Somewhere between these two extremes the truth must lie. It is an undoubted fact that the Sophists did more harm by their teaching than most of them ever intended; but then that charge could, with some plausibility, also be levelled at Socrates. Some, like Thrasymachus of Chalcedon, were might-is-right extremists. Others, such as Protagoras (died *c.* 420) seem to have been earnest rationalists, with an oddly Victorian tinge of progressive optimism about them. He held that in a civilized *polis* even the worst citizen was already morally and intellectually superior to any noble savage. Before his death he had good grounds for discarding so naive a view. 'Faith in the inevitability of progress', as Dodds well remarked, 'had an even shorter run in Athens than in England'.

Many of the Sophists offered to teach anything from music to mathematics. For the most part, however, they concentrated on *areté*, an almost untranslatable word (often misleadingly rendered as 'virtue') which suggests the full life, the complete development of a person's natural powers and talents. This, as C. M. Bowra pointed out, 'all too easily became a study of worldly success'. Men who could afford to take lessons from the Sophists were determined to make their mark by way of politics and the law-courts. What *they* wanted, and would pay good money for, was a training in rhetoric – the forceful presentation of a case, the unscrupulous exploitation of logic. However much the Sophists may have prided themselves (and some did) on holding aloof from politics, the weapons they put into the hands of ambitious young men were to prove immensely effective.

Their theories, moreover, could all too easily be perverted for partisan ends. This applies in particular to the famous antithesis they propounded between *nomos* and *physis*, generally translated as 'law' (or 'custom') and 'nature'. Both terms were dangerously ambiguous. *Nomos* could be anything from inherited tradition to the man-made laws of *polis* or *tyrannos*. *Physis* was an even more explosive concept, and a godsend to would-be imperialists or dictators. It was only too easy for those who rejected *nomos* (*qua* human sanctions) to extrapolate arguments for 'natural rights' based on the law of the jungle – which is, in one sense, incontrovertibly 'natural'. Might is right, the conclusion will run: nature looks kindly on the survival of the fittest. Such arguments are by no means dead today. One good reason for studying the Sophists is that the topics they raised – law versus morality, the social compact, the unity of mankind – still have the power to arouse and divide modern society: they are perennial.

The undoubted decline in Athenian morality towards the close of the fifth century is most often attributed to a mixture of war exhaustion, plague and demagoguery. But acting as a yeast – or a dissolvent – behind such public phenomena was a cluster of related *ideas*, stimulating heterodoxy, breaking down traditional social and moral restraints. If the Athenians could commit genocide on Melos in 416 it was (as Thucydides makes clear) a perversion of the *nomos-physis* argument which provided them with their justification. As early as 431, when refusing to relinquish their imperial power, they had declared through an official spokesman: 'It has always been a rule that the weak should be subject to the strong; and besides, we are worthy of our power.' Such arguments the man-in-the-street probably swallowed without qualms; everyone enjoys being on the winning side. But when it came to religious traditionalism his reaction was significantly different.

The climate of 'progressive' thought engendered by the Sophists aroused a fierce, and fiercely emotional, resentment among pious conservatives and the common people in Athens. The result was a kind of book-burning drive against atheists and heretics, a pre-Christian Inquisition. We hear a good deal – though never enough in detail – about the various witch-hunting 'impiety trials' held between 438 and 399, against the shadow and backwash of the Peloponnesian War. Apart from a marginal figure like Aspasia, all the victims were distinguished artists or intellectuals: Pheidias, Anaxagoras, Diagoras the Melian, Protagoras, and, of course, Socrates. Aristophanes, in *The Clouds* (423), offers a glimpse of just what the New Learning meant to ordinary people in social terms. Radical opinions could be perilous for those who held them. From Plato's dialogue *Protagoras* we learn that the Sophists were often obliged to teach privately as a safeguard against informers. Not only disbelief in the supernatural, but also the teaching of astronomy and meteorology were made indictable offences. Where, now, was the old romantic myth of Athenian *parrhesia*, freedom of thought and expression? By systematically challenging all the old religious, social and intellectual shibboleths, the Sophists were risking more than they knew. Every intellectual advance must be bought at a price. In fifth-century Athens that price included a powerful wave of bigotry, hysteria and repressive violence, which seemingly interminable warfare merely served to swell.

The Archidamian War and the phoney peace

Athens went to war in 431 with the kind of blithe arrogant confidence which marked the American Confederacy in 1860 or the British upper classes in 1914. She had a first-class fleet, an enormous cash reserve, and what, at the time, seemed bright prospects of victory. If the Peloponnesian League could be eliminated as an obstacle once and for all, Athens' imperial destiny stood secure. Yet Pericles must have been well aware how appallingly expensive such a war was bound to prove. The Samian Revolt (440), which cost over twelve hundred talents for a couple of seasons' fighting, made it all too clear that a long-drawn-out struggle was liable to cripple Athens financially. The actual record of the first ten years' hostilities amply confirms such a supposition. On economic grounds, then, Pericles must have calculated war as the lesser of two evils. A showdown with Sparta and her allies might depreciate Athens' reserves; but unless she secured reliable overseas markets, especially for grain and timber, there was a real danger of the economy collapsing altogether.

Granted these facts, it is hard to understand the strategy which Pericles imposed on Athens during the first years of the war: in military, economic and psychological terms alike it can only be accounted sheer disaster. He would not, under any circumstances, let an Athenian hoplite force meet Sparta's warriors in the field. Instead, he evacuated Attica altogether, brought the country population inside the Long Walls and let the Spartans ravage Athenian fields and farms as the Persians had done, without raising a hand to stop them. Meanwhile, the Athenian fleet conducted ineffectual raids round the Peloponnese, while the Athenian army (carefully waiting until the Spartans had gone home) made gingerly incursions into the Megarid. How this inconclusive fish-and-fox campaigning was supposed to win the war for Athens is anyone's guess; but there can be little doubt as to its appalling effect on public morale. It is symptomatic of how far Athens had moved away from the old landowning ideal since Marathon that such a scheme could have been implemented at all.

Attica had only within the last few years recovered from the devasta-tion caused by the Persian Wars. To abandon vines and olives and farms that had absorbed heavy investment before they even began to show a profit again meant a huge and deliberate economic sacrifice. Worse, the tacit admission that an Athenian hoplite was not thought capable of beating his Spartan opposite number in fair fight could scarcely improve Athens' will to win. But the most appalling hazard of all, a direct result of those thousands of refugees from the countryside being cooped up in horrible shacks between the Long Walls, was a plague epidemic: probably bubonic, though typhus and measles have also been suggested. The disease struck Athens early in 430, having reached Piraeus, it would seem, aboard a grain-ship. It ran rampant for about a year, killing something like one quarter of the entire population. There was another minor outbreak in the winter of 427/6.

Between the outbreak of war and autumn 429, when he died of the plague himself, Pericles' policy had little to show for it but heavy casualty-lists, burnt-out farms, rebellious allies and increasingly poor morale. In this context the famous Funeral Oration – pronounced over the victims of the first year's fighting – takes on a curiously macabre quality. But with Pericles' death, and the emergence of Cleon – a merchant-tanner and radical demagogue immortalized by the attacks of Aristophanes – a new vigour and dynamism can be detected in Athenian strategy: a new brutality, too. How far this change was due to that collapse of public morality induced (Thucy-dides tells us) by the plague is a difficult point to decide. The sheer length of the war may have had something to do with it; both sides began to commit atrocities as time wore on. Citizen-soldiers had never before been required to face sustained and heavy losses over so long a period, and (if we can believe numerous allusions in the comic poets) there was a marked increase in desertion and draft-dodging as the struggle dragged on.

In 427, after a two-year siege, the Spartans captured Plataea, Athens' one serious Boeotian ally, and proceeded to slaughter all citizens who could not prove pro-Spartan activities during the war. (Could any? one wonders.) That same year saw the collapse of an anti-Athenian rebellion on the large and powerful island of Lesbos. When the rebels surrendered, Cleon forced through a motion calling for the execution of all adult males, the enslavement of all women and children. In the nick of time, the order was rescinded – though not, we may note, on humanitarian grounds. Genocide, the argument ran, made bad war propaganda, and would create more problems than it solved. Pericles, it has been suggested, would never have behaved with such ruthless-ness. But then Pericles was never exposed to the harsh necessities of total war which arose in the years after 429. On the other hand, his conduct during the reduction of Samos in 440 had shown he could be tough enough when the need arose, and by the end of his life (if we can believe Thucydides) he had reached an attitude of total cynicism about Athens' imperial ambitions.

Something of his grim dilemma may be reflected in Sophocles' most famous play, *Oedipus the King*, produced about this time. The opening scene, with its description of a plague-stricken Thebes, can-not but reflect Athens' own experiences. This leads one to wonder how far a pious conservative like Sophocles automatically assumed that such a visitation must be the direct outcome (as at Thebes in his play) of some great offence, public or private: *ate* overtaking *hubris*, divine punishment for human error. Perhaps there is a more fundamental allusion, too, to the central problem of the epoch. Oedipus, though not essentially a hubristic figure, does very much pride himself on applying human reason to life at all levels. Sophocles stood by the old divine laws. The conflict was basic, and it may not be altogether fanciful to see in this rational hero, destroyed by a Fate which steadily shreds his will and reason, some allusion to Pericles' own grim end, struck down by what many must have seen as the hand of God for morethanmortal presumption.

Cleon remained in charge of Athens' war policy while he lived, which was for the best part of the socalled 'Archidamian War' (431–421), concluded by the Peace of Nicias, and named after the Spartan King, Archidamus, who conducted annual raids into Attica during its early years. That policy concerned itself, for the most part, with overhauling Athenian finances, blockading the Peloponnese and seeking new sources of grain and timber. It was during this period that notions of western expansionism, involving Sicily or southern Italy, first began to gain currency at Athens. The singularly bloody civil war fought out on Corcyra (Corfu) in 427 makes very good sense when we realize that this great island, the Gibraltar of the Adriatic, formed the key to the western searoute: no wonder both sides fought and intrigued so savagely for its possession. The first, abortive Sicilian expedition launched by Athens (427–424) also takes on greater significance in this context.

174–6 Top left: obverse of silver stater from Poseidonia (Paestum), Magna Graecia (540 BC) showing Poseidon, wearing a chlamys, and with poised trident. To his left, the Greek letters POS. Below left: reverse of silver tetradrachm from Acragas (Agrigento), *c.* 420–415 BC. Above, the crab, emblem of Acragas (as the seaturtle was of Aegina); below, Scylla, the monster that traditionally haunted the Straits of Messina, shown here with seaserpent's tail and dogs barking from her groin. Right: three Syracusan coins, two showing the head of Arethusa, with dolphins, the third depicting the Syracusan fourhorse chariot (quadriga), *c.* 485 BC.

177 Opposite: map of Sicily and Magna Graecia.

ADRIATIC

SEA

ITALY

Bari

Brundisium

APENNINES

Cumae *Neapolis*

Taras (Tarentum)

Metapontum

Paestum

Sele

Velia

Agri

Heraclea

GULF OF TARAS

TYRRHENIAN

Sybaris

Thurii

SEA

Croton

Terina

Aeolian Islands

Caulonia

Locri

Lipara

Zancle-Messina

Panormus(Palermo)
Soluntum (Solus)

Rhegium

IONIAN

Eryx

Sicily

Etna

Naxos

Segesta

Himera

Hadranum

Hypsas

Centuripe

Catana

SEA

Enna

Halycus

Symaethus

Selinus

Acragas (Agrigento)

Leontini

Gelas

Megara Hyblaea

Syracuse

Gela

Camarina

Melita(Malta)

| 0 | 25 | 50 | 75 | 100 MIS |
| 0 | 40 | 80 | 120 | 160 Kms |

178 A view of Paestum, with the Temple of Hera I, the so-called 'Basilica', on the right.

179 The Doric Temple of Segesta, north-west Sicily (425–409 BC). Segesta, or Egesta, was an Elymite city-state which achieved fame by appealing to Athens for help against her neighbour and rival, Selinus (416 BC), thus precipitating the Sicilian Expedition.

180 Acragas (Agrigento), southern Sicily: in the background, the Doric temples known (traditionally but misleadingly) as those of 'Hercules' (late sixth century BC) and Concord (late fifth century BC), the latter well preserved through use as a Christian church. In the foreground, the ruins of the gigantic Temple of Zeus – originally over 173 by 361 feet, with columns 13 feet in diameter and 120 feet high (fifth century BC).

181 The Greek theatre of Syracuse (in its present form built c. 230 BC by Hieron II), and beyond it, to the south, the Great Harbour. The oldest theatre in Syracuse (known as the 'Linear Theatre' because of its design) lies a little to the south-west.

182 Relief on Greek grave-stone (? Attica, late fifth century BC) commemorating the death of a soldier: the combatants may be an Athenian and a Spartan during the Peloponnesian War.

Meanwhile the war at home entered a new phase. The capture of 120 full Spartiate warriors at Sphacteria in 425 gave Athens a chance to obtain a negotiated peace. Cleon rejected this opportunity, obviously hoping for unconditional surrender. After this Athens' position deteriorated. The Spartan general Brasidas first occupied Megara, then made a lightning dash through Thessaly and Thrace to capture the Athenian port of Amphipolis – which gave access not only to valuable timber-supplies, but also to the gold-mines of Mount Pangaeus. In 424 the Athenians suffered a sharp defeat at Delium – almost the only true land-battle fought during the Archidamian War. However, in 422 both Cleon and Brasidas were killed during an unsuccessful attempt to recapture Amphipolis. With the two most hawkish leaders on each side thus removed, both Sparta and Athens set about working out terms for a final peace settlement. This was signed in spring 421, the chief negotiators being King Pleistoanax of Sparta and the pious Athenian mine-owner Nicias, by whose name the fifty-year treaty is still known.

There was a great deal of excitement and rejoicing – premature, as it turned out – among the war-weary populace. Euripides wrote a famous passage in his lost play *Erechtheus* beginning: 'Down with my spear, let it be covered with spiders' webs!' But the Peace of Nicias solved nothing: it was simply a confession of temporary physical and financial exhaustion by both sides. New faces, too, began to emerge: most notably, Pericles' raffish young ward Alcibiades, an ambitious politician whose racing-stable, pet quail and scandalous affairs made him the talk of the town. Nicias and Alcibiades came to symbolize the old and the new Athens during these inter-war years: middle-of-the-road pro-Spartan conservatism versus expansionist diplomacy based on alliance with Argos, a Peloponnesian bloc that would isolate Sparta and finally bring her down. The Argive coalition collapsed in 418, when Sparta scored a sharp victory over Athenian-backed Argive forces at Mantinea; but Alcibiades' anti-Spartan expansionist policy lingered on with remarkable persistence. The younger generation in particular took it up with unbounded enthusiasm. War, to them, meant guaranteed employment and the prospect of rich pickings abroad – an almost irresistible combination.

By 416, indeed, Alcibiades was back on the Board of Generals (a position he had lost after the Mantinea débâcle), having meanwhile gained much popularity by winning first, second and fourth places with his chariot-teams at the Olympic Games. In that same year

183, 184 Olympia: above, the starting-line in the stadium; right, passage leading to the stadium.

Athens embarked on a campaign against the little island of Melos, which arguably owed her no allegiance at all. This is made by Thucydides the occasion for inserting in his *History* a dialogue between spokesmen for Melos and Athens, the latter expressing the might-is-right *physis* ethic in its most naked form. No second thoughts this time; the genocide was duly carried out, and Alcibiades voted for it. Then, with dramatic aptness, the very instrument of fate, there reached Athens an embassy from a small, insignificant town in Sicily, Segesta, asking for help and alliance. The chain of circumstances which that embassy set in motion ran its course three years later, by a blood-sodden Sicilian river, with the destruction of the proudest expeditionary force ever to sail from Piraeus.

Unconditional surrender

By 416 Athens had largely recovered from the effects of plague, if not of war. Population, trade and actual wealth were booming: the number of slaves, too, had risen. On the other hand, since no sure source of grain or timber had been established within the empire, the economic situation as a whole still remained precarious. Thus the prospect of rich pickings in the west now looked vastly attractive. Sicily in particular had acquired quasi-mythical features for the average Athenian, who saw it as a kind of Cockaigne or Eldorado, where fabulous loot was not only to be had, but had for the asking. This scheme of profitable treasure-hunting was associated with the radical front, now split into two mutually hostile groups. One was led by Cleon's successors Hyperbolus, a lamp-maker, and Androcles: urban entrepreneurs or artisans who specialized in sharp litigation and populist demagoguery. The other was associated with smart young aristocrats such as Phaeax or Alcibiades, the 'New Progressives' attacked by Aristophanes in his earliest play, *The Banqueters*.

If Alcibiades was, as Plutarch says, dreaming of vast western conquests, so, undoubtedly, were Hyperbolus and his business associates: the vast swarm of traders and speculators which accompanied Athens' expeditionary force to Sicily makes that clear enough. When Segesta's ambassadors gave Athens the diplomatic opening she needed to interfere in Sicily, Hyperbolus made up his mind to get rid of so dangerous a rival. He therefore proposed an ostracism (?415). Never did a political scheme backfire more disastrously. Deep called to gentlemanly deep: Alcibiades, Phaeax and Nicias reached a private agreement behind the scenes, and so organized matters that when the ostracism was held, *all* their followers voted against Hyperbolus himself, who was thus (in George Forrest's immortal phrase) hoist with his own potsherd. The affair made a nine days' joke in Athens, but afterwards people came to feel that the whole institution

185 Athenian *ostraka* (fifth century BC), inscribed with names including those of Aristeides, Lysimachus (possibly Aristeides' father: his son, of the same name, never achieved prominence in public life), Themistocles and Pericles.

186 Detail of a black bowl (red-figure, fifth century) showing a sculptor carving a herm.

of ostracism had been degraded by it. So a political instrument which had numbered Cimon and Themistocles among its victims was now formally abolished.

Intellectuals like Euripides might have qualms about genocide on Melos, as *The Trojan Women* (415) makes clear; but the prospect of raping Sicily aroused nothing but enthusiasm among expansionists, and purely *practical* objections from conservatives or moderates. Moral scruples they had none; all that concerned them was whether this legitimate imperialist venture could succeed – a fear which, in the event, proved all too justifiable. A commission of inquiry returned from Segesta with tales of conspicuous affluence (afterwards supposedly revealed as fraudulent, but this may have been Athenian propaganda to justify the expedition's patent lack of interest in Segestan affairs). On the basis of their report a sixty-ship squadron was voted 'to help the Segestans against the Selinuntines . . . and in general to make the kind of provisions for Sicily which might seem to them most in accordance with Athenian interests' (Thucydides, Bk. VI) – a convenient holdall clause.

Four days later that cautious figure Nicias, one of the three commanders-designate, made a blistering attack on the expedition as such, claiming (what of course was true) that 'the city was in fact aiming at conquering the whole of Sicily'. The Assembly, ignoring his objections, voted him a larger fleet. Foiled in debate, Nicias whipped up various seers and diviners to prophesy doom for the venture, while Alcibiades, nothing daunted, hired rival oracles predicting glorious Athenian triumphs. During the night of 6/7 June 415, an anonymous but well-organized group of iconoclasts went round Athens systematically defacing those square-pillar busts of Hermes which stood at street corners. In some irrational way people convinced themselves that here was 'evidence of a revolutionary conspiracy to overthrow the democracy'. The mutilation of the Herms could in fact have had only one motive: to secure an omen bad enough to stop the fleet from sailing. In this it failed; but the populists used it (reinforced with a blasphemy charge) to smear Alcibiades, who found himself in the anomalous position of sailing for Sicily with a capital indictment outstanding against him.

Athens' great armada finally reached Sicily in the late summer of 415, and its commanders at once began to show signs of that indecisiveness, lack of initiative and plain incompetence which marked the entire campaign. Alcibiades, on being recalled to stand trial, jumped ship at Thurii and deserted to Sparta, where he fed the Spartans lethally good advice on how to defeat his own fellow countrymen – including the dispatch of a Spartan general to conduct anti-Athenian operations in Sicily, and the permanent occupation of

187 Notice of the sale of Alcibiades' property after his condemnation (414 BC) in connection with the profanation of the Mysteries and mutilation of the Herms. The list includes, *inter alia*, ten Milesian beds and six perfume-jars.

Decelea in Attica. With the death of the third commander, Lamachus, the sick and dilatory Nicias was left in sole charge of the expeditionary force. In spring 414 Aristophanes' play *The Birds* could satirize the Sicilian venture as a fantastic airborne imperial development scheme, a racket run for crooks, profiteers and fiddling bureaucrats. Little more than a year later (September 413), after an appalling series of disasters, the entire Athenian expeditionary force in Sicily was wiped out during an overland retreat. Over twenty-nine thousand men, up to two hundred of the city's best triremes, and perhaps four thousand talents in cash had been squandered for nothing. To cap everything else, King Agis of Sparta now occupied Decelea, as Alcibiades had suggested: a move which led eventually to the closure of the Laurium mines and the desertion of up to twenty thousand slaves.

Athens rallied as best she could. The political climate (as so often after a major defeat: compare the Germany of the Weimar Republic) began to change in favour of right-wing extremism. Ten commissioners of Public Safety (*probouloi*) were appointed to 'advise' the Council. Work on the Erechtheum, begun after the Peace of Nicias (421), was temporarily suspended. An emergency shipbuilding programme was launched, and only just in time: the spring of 412 brought a rash of revolts by the Ionian subject-allies, largely at Alcibiades' instigation. While Euripides in the *Helen* noted man's inability to decide 'what is god or not god or something in between', the elderly comedian Eupolis produced his last play, *The Demes*, in which great statesmen of the past, from Solon to Pericles, were raised from the dead to guide the *polis* in its hour of crisis. This psychological tendency to turn back the clock became increasingly marked as the war dragged on, reaching its climax with the contest between Aeschylus and Euripides in *The Frogs*.

In 411 a group of right-wing revolutionaries launched a coup in Athens based on that nostalgic if vague reactionary ideal, the 'ancestral constitution'. After a moderate start, this junta, the so-called 'Four Hundred', set about running Athens on vigorously totalitarian lines, with something very like a reign of terror. The Athenian fleet was away at Samos (one reason why the coup had succeeded), and its commanders, learning what was afoot back home, promptly formed a democratic government-in-exile. They also recalled Alcibiades, who by this time had a Spartan price on his head (King Agis, whose wife he had seduced, wore horns less peaceably than most men), and was involved in tortuous diplomacy with the Persian satraps of Ionia to secure the Great King's backing. Alcibiades earned his country's grateful thanks by stopping the fleet from sailing back to Piraeus against the junta, and thus precipitating a full-scale civil war. Instead he more usefully led them from one victory to another against the Peloponnesian fleet (now much expanded with Persian support), culminating in an engagement off Cyzicus (May 410) which for the moment ended all organized naval opposition in the eastern Aegean.

Meanwhile the Four Hundred had fallen for lack of support, to be replaced by a more moderate regime, based on the original scheme for an elite franchise of five thousand (both Thucydides and Aristotle praise this constitution highly, a significant pointer). One immediate consequence of Cyzicus, however, was the restoration of full democracy, under a new urban demagogue, a lyre-maker named Cleophon. Sparta made Athens a peace-offer on the basis of the *status quo*; the Assembly, at Cleophon's urging, turned it down flat. The question of Alcibiades' return occupied all minds. There was still deep resentment against him, but, equally, a feeling that nobody else could win the war. Over forty now, the eternal playboy still retained some of his old quasi-Periclean charisma. But he did not dare risk a return (even though it had been voted in the Assembly) for another two years: years during which he notched up further dazzling victories by way of amends for past conduct, including the recapture of Chalcedon and Byzantium on the Bosporus. It was not until the summer of 407 – by which time Athens was so short of silver that she had been reduced to melting down her gold images and utensils into currency – that Alcibiades staged a triumphal return to his native city.

He had timed things well. His property was restored, the Athenian priesthood revoked the curses they had laid on him and he was appointed Supreme Commander-in-Chief. To symbolize his reconciliation with the gods, he personally provided a cavalry escort for the sacred procession from Eleusis, discontinued since the Spartan capture of Decelea. Yet he knew, better than anyone, that his rehabilitation, as far as the *demos* was concerned, stood or fell by continued military successes. One failure, and he was lost. The moment came all too soon. In the winter of 407/6, while he was drumming up pay for his troops, his deputy – disobeying orders – suffered a defeat off Notium. Alcibiades, deposed from his command, wisely chose exile rather than justification before the Assembly, and retreated to a castle he had bought for himself in the Thracian Chersonese. About the same time, in Athens, the nonagenarian Sophocles dressed his chorus in mourning for Euripides' death. The old landmarks were fast vanishing.

With indestructible optimism, Athens built yet another fleet from good Macedonian timber (paid for this time by melting down Acropolis dedications) and scored a great victory off the Arginusae Islands, near Mytilene (406). Unfortunately a storm blew up, and the captains failed to save numerous sailors from the water. For this they were prosecuted, in an atmosphere of hysterical fury, and put to death. Sparta once more made peace proposals, but Cleophon – storming into the Assembly drunk, in full armour – got these overtures, too, rejected. After a vain warning from Alcibiades, who left his castle to remonstrate with them for the position they had taken up, the commanders of Athens' last fleet were totally defeated by the Spartan admiral Lysander at Aegospotami, the 'Goat River', opposite Lampsacus on what is now the Gallipoli peninsula. After a winter (405/4) of starvation under siege, Athens at last surrendered. 'It was thought,' Xenophon wrote, 'that this day was the beginning of freedom for Greece.' It certainly marked the end of an era.

188 Marble stele from the Acropolis: relief showing Athena and Hera, the patron goddesses of Athens and Samos respectively, standing with hands clasped in token of alliance. Below (not seen here), the words 'Cephisophon, of Paeania, was secretary', which dates the stele to 403/2, after the fall of the Thirty Tyrants: it nevertheless commemorates a decree, honouring the loyal Samians, passed in 405, shortly before the fall of Athens. The text followed.

147

5

The reversion to authoritarianism (404–323 BC)

The decline of the polis: Aegospotami to Mantinea

It took very little time for those who had heralded the dawn of Greek freedom in 404 to realize that they had simply exchanged one despotism for another, which did not even possess its predecessor's merits of intelligence, brilliance and style. This was true, not only of Sparta, the paramount Greek state between 404 and 371, but also of her successor Thebes (371–362). The Theban general Epaminondas once said it was his ambition to bring the Athenian Propylaea to the Cadmeia, Thebes' acropolis: that went to the heart of the matter, but as a programme was doomed to failure. There was no longer an Alcman at Sparta; there was no longer a Pindar in Thebes. Both regimes made themselves notorious through their rigidity, authoritarianism, wanton aggression and atrocities. The general pattern of each is only emphasized by their striking exceptions, such as Pelopidas or Epaminondas himself (Agesilaus and Lysander are hardly advertisements for culture). One ends by suspecting that Aristophanes' vaudeville jokes about the thick Doric mentality may have a grain of truth as well as Attic salt in them.

Sparta hardly got off to a good start after the war. It is true that the effects of Athenian imperialism were reversed wherever possible: Aegina and Melos regained their independence, the *cleruchs* were expelled, the exiles reinstated. But this counted for little against the brutal behaviour of Spartan-backed *decarchies* (ten-man juntas) all over the Aegean. Nor did anyone forget that, during the final phase of the Peloponnesian War, the Spartans had bargained away the Greek cities of Asia Minor to the Great King in return for much-needed gold and other subventions – an act which made their claim to have been fighting for Greek freedom look a trifle shop-soiled. Worst of all was

189 Silver tetradrachm from Egypt minted *c.* 305 BC by Ptolemy I: obverse showing Alexander the Great wearing elephant scalp and the ram's horns of Zeus Ammon.

the totalitarian coup which took place in Athens itself. A government of thirty picked oligarchs was established (September 404). This bully-boy group, backed by Lysander's Spartan garrison on the Acropolis, zestfully set about eliminating all opposition by means of a series of purges. Some fifteen hundred 'unreliable elements' were executed, including a number of wealthy resident aliens whom the Thirty put to death simply as a means of laying hands on some ready cash.

About five hundred democrats fled the country, to become the nucleus of a resistance group based on Thebes. By September 403 the extremists had lost control in Athens, and finally withdrew to Eleusis, where they set up an independent state. Lysander's tough line was beginning to lose its attraction even in Sparta, and he now found himself superseded. By the winter of 403/2 Athens had once more become a full democracy. The *ultras* held out at Eleusis till 400, when their leaders were lured to a conference and done away with. The remainder then received a general amnesty. It had been an extremely unpleasant, not to say traumatic period, the scars of which took years to heal, and left their legacy of hatred and fear and suspicion. The word 'oligarch', like 'fascist' in our own day, was now an automatic insult. The fear, moreover, extended, in a hysterical fashion, to those social and intellectual circles in which the more high-powered extremists had moved. This was the atmosphere surrounding the trial and condemnation of Socrates (399). Behind the old philosopher stood the ghosts of his two most famous pupils: Alcibiades (executed by the Persians in 404 at Lysander's request), and the leader of the Thirty, Critias (also, incidentally, Plato's cousin). One can scarcely wonder at the verdict.

Sparta emerges from the next three decades as perhaps the most inept state ever to hold a leading position in Greece. Isolationist, old-fashioned, autocratic, and terrified of overseas commitments, her ruling class could hardly have been more grotesquely unsuited for the task of running a large ex-empire. Once Spartans were let off the leash of discipline abroad they became corrupt and avaricious petty tyrants. The Spartan government exacted tribute in much the same way as Athens had done, though with even more brutal methods of collection. One thousand talents per annum was the reputed sum, and Sparta's Peloponnesian allies never saw a penny of it. Thus within a very short space of time she had managed to alienate both Athens' old subject-allies and her own loyal supporters: a remarkable exercise in diplomatic tactlessness. Perhaps hoping to wipe out the moral stigma which her deal with Persia had produced, she also backed the ill-fated rebellion by the Great King's brother, Cyrus, which collapsed after the Battle of Cunaxa, near Babylon (401).

This débâcle is chiefly remembered for the subsequent retreat up-country of no less than ten thousand Greek mercenaries to the Black Sea and eventual safety – a feat duly commemorated by one of their commanders, Xenophon the Athenian, in his *Anabasis*. The episode drew considerable attention to Persia's undoubted military weaknesses. From now on the notion of uniting all leading Greek states in a crusade against 'the Barbarian' became steadily more popular. One of its most zealous advocates was Isocrates (436–338), educationalist and political pamphleteer, especially in an eloquent tract entitled *Panegyricus* (380). It is one of fate's choicer ironies that the man who eventually made Isocrates' dreams come true, Alexander (*see* pp. 163 ff.), was a half-Epirot, half-Macedonian conqueror whom civilized Greeks, rightly or wrongly, regarded as a barbarian himself.

Throughout the first decade of the fourth century Sparta and Persia continued to spar uneasily, while Athens worked steadily to restore her naval authority in the Aegean. An anti-Spartan coalition now developed among the Greek states; Persia (perhaps remembering Alcibiades' cynical advice) decided to play each side off against the other. By 393, just over ten years after their demolition, the Long Walls were rebuilt – with Persian gold. Another four years, and Athens was in a position to restore her old 5 per cent toll on seagoing freight. Both Sparta and Persia seem to have regarded this resurgence of Athens' naval power, understandably, with some alarm. The result was the so-called 'King's Peace' (387/6), which finally restored the Ionian littoral to Persia, and insisted on all other Greek cities (with one or two unimportant exceptions) retaining their autonomy – a measure aimed chiefly at breaking up Athens' new Aegean federation, and Thebes' equally dangerous hegemony over Boeotia.

This Persian-dictated settlement was regarded, rightly, as an insult by the Greek-speaking world, and its brutal enforcement by King Agesilaus of Sparta merely served to crystallize a determined opposition to Spartan overlordship. Thebes and Athens were thrown into alliance, and both acted with flagrant disregard of the terms of the King's Peace. Athens proceeded to float what is known as the 'Second Athenian Confederacy', a maritime league which soon equalled that of her palmy fifth-century days, and included most of the same members. Thebes, similarly, rebuilt her Boeotian federation, and carried through extensive military reforms (including the establishment of a full-time professional infantry regiment, the Sacred Band). In the sporadic war which ensued both cities gave Sparta a very rough time of it. There were abortive invasions and patched-up truces. Funds began to run short all round, and a showdown of some sort became essential. In June 371 a treaty was drafted between Athens, Thebes and Sparta; but when Thebes insisted on signing for *all* Boeotian cities (a *de facto* recognition of her land-empire) negotiations collapsed, and King Cleombrotus of Sparta at once invaded Boeotia in force.

The Spartan army met that of Thebes at Leuctra (July 371). Epaminondas packed one wing – contrary to all accepted usages of war – forty shields deep; since an ancient infantry engagement more or less resembled a football scrum, he managed to roll up the Spartan line by sheer superior weight. The result was a total and absolute victory for Thebes, which broke Sparta's hold on Greece overnight, and abolished the last lingering traces of myth about the invincibility of the Spartan war-machine. Thebes thus had an opportunity to assume the leadership of Greece, but in the event muffed it almost as badly as Sparta had done. The decade sputtered out in a bewildering series of land- and sea-battles, inconclusive campaigns, small and

190, 191 Opposite, top: bronze relief plaque found on a chest in Pompeii: thought to represent Diotima (or Aspasia), Eros and Socrates, but all three attributions are dubious. Below: Roman copy of a late fourth-century portrait-bust of Isocrates, representing him in his prime (he lived to be a near-centenarian). Scholars have commented on the shyness and imaginative vision suggested by this likeness – very much in line with what we know of his life.

temporary triumphs. No Greek state, it seemed, was now capable of setting the rest a true lead. The Theban venture proved a mere repetition, under somewhat better leadership, of Sparta's disastrous essay in militaristic imperialism.

This realization eventually led to a coalition of Sparta, Athens, Elis, Achaea and Mantinea against Thebes. At the Battle of Mantinea (362) Thebes' forces scored a decisive victory, but at the last minute failed to consolidate their advantage – indeed, went to pieces – because of Epaminondas' death. He alone had been the architect of their triumph; when the head was cut off, the body could do nothing. The Greek states at once relapsed into separatism and chaos. Athens had a stronger fleet than under the Periclean regime, but made singularly little use of it. Sparta retreated into surly isolationism. And then, a year or two later (359), there came to the throne of a country which every Greek statesman had hitherto discounted – Macedonia – one of the most remarkable monarchs in European history. With the accession of Philip II, Greek affairs abruptly reassume a shape and a pattern: the dominating pattern of one man with an obsession, and the will to win.

192, 193 Opposite, top: detail of the so-called 'Nereid Monument' from Xanthus, Lycia (now reconstructed in the British Museum): frieze on a pediment, showing warriors in battle. This monument 'was actually a tomb in the form of an Ionic temple on a very tall base' (A.W. Lawrence, *Greek and Roman Sculpture*). Below: detail of the 'Lenormant relief' from the Erechtheum, Athens (c. 400 BC) showing the forward hull section of the starboard side of a trireme, with deck-stanchions, outrigger and oars in place.

194 A gold coin (obverse) of Philip II, showing Zeus: the model is likely to be Philip himself.

153

The metamorphosis of reality

We are so bedazzled by the particular creative achievements of the Periclean Age that it is easy for us, not only to neglect that age's failings, but also seriously to underrate what came after, on the grounds that anything else could not help being an anticlimax. The High Classical pattern becomes a yardstick of perfection (this process began even before Aristotle's day) against which all other artistic or political phenomena are measured and found wanting. Hence the popular but erroneous theory of general cultural decline from the fourth century onwards. It is true that there were certain characteristic things which the Periclean *polis* did supremely well, and which never achieved comparable stature thereafter: the most obvious example is Attic drama. As early as 386 a law was passed stating that one play by the three 'Old Masters' – Aeschylus, Sophocles, Euripides – had to be revived annually. Athens, clearly, had reached a point all too familiar to contemporary society, that of being intimidated by her own classics.

195 Opposite: the ransom of Hector, a scene from Aeschylus' *Phrygians*, detail of a terracotta relief from Melos (*c.* 440 BC). Priam, who has brought gold to be weighed against the body of Hector, is seen on the right, his hand to his forehead. On the left, Achilles, wearing a corselet; Hector's body lies on the ground.

196 Left: a comic actor portraying a slave carrying a basket to an altar, shown on a red-figure phlyax vase (fourth century BC).

By the mid fourth century in the *Poetics* Aristotle was looking back to a play like Sophocles' *Oedipus* as the 'ideal' type of Attic tragedy. The critical mood was retrospective, nostalgic, a celebration of the past. The genre, in fact, had died; now all that remained was to typologize and embalm it.

An equally striking metamorphosis can be detected in comedy. So vast a watershed lies between Aristophanes' early plays, *e.g. The Knights* (424), and his last work, the *Plutus* (388) that it is hard to believe they are by the same hand. Gone, as though they had never existed, are the gay, arrogant self-confidence and savage political satire; gone, too, are the marvellous choral odes. The *Plutus* contains, in embryo, all the basic ingredients of what, under Menander (342–?290), was to become New Comedy – an increased emphasis on domestic trivia and personal relationships, a lack of public or political motivation (though the *Plutus* does contain social criticism of a sort, *e.g.* that poverty is good inasmuch as it makes a man work for his daily bread rather than for luxuries), the tendency towards superstition and thaumaturgy, the obsession with Fortune (*Tyche*), the cult of affluent urban individualism. Here, in short, we see a foreshadowing of the Hellenistic era.

Such a picture, clearly, reflects profound social and psychological changes in the *polis* where drama had come to maturity; but to claim that it indicates decline is to beg the question. For various reasons the emphasis of interest, the temper of mind, had changed. We find no falling off in creativity or imagination, which are, rather, now directed into somewhat different channels. Just as the fifth century had emphasized the dialectic of drama, the visual celebration of the *polis* through sculpture and architecture, the collective (or, in the widest sense, political) core of artistic expression, so the fourth turned to what, in essence, we may describe as an intellectual or academic approach. This was the age of great philosophers and thinkers, of developments in mathematics and astronomy, law and criticism. It was the great age of prose rather than poetry, of urban centres and individuals rather than the limited collective of the *polis* – though sentimental attachment to the *polis* ideal, especially among intellectuals, long outlasted the *polis* itself as an effective instrument of government.

197–200 Examples of fourth-century and Hellenistic jewellery: elaborate gold ear-pendants from Crispiano, near Taranto (below, left and centre); a gold grid pin (below right); and two gold bracelets terminating in dog and lion heads, from Ginosa (opposite).

What brought about so radical a change? It is often said that Athens' loss of imperial hegemony in 404 somehow broke her spirit, that the Peloponnesian War left a traumatic scar on the collective Athenian psyche. At a deep level this might conceivably be true, but it will not serve as a general explanation. Serious curtailment of political freedom began only in 338, with Philip of Macedon's victory over the Greek states at Chaeronea. Yet characteristic symptoms of supposed 'decline' (traditionally associated with loss of democratic freedom) had begun to appear by the 380s, if not earlier, when the Athenian *demos* was at its most unbridled, and Athens had embarked on a spirited attempt to regain her old sea-empire. Two factors, however, which undoubtedly *did* have an immediate effect on the psychological climate and popular ethics were the intellectual legacy of the Sophists, and the marked swing from agriculturalism towards an urban-based import-export economy. The first, by emphasizing man's intellectual autonomy and preaching ethical neutralism, both undermined traditional collective values and encouraged self-knowledge (which easily led to self-preoccupation) in the individual. The second augmented this trend by increasing the gross national wealth (with a resultant emphasis on luxuries, duly noted in the *Plutus*) and producing

a large class of city-dwellers who had little attachment either to the land or to the values which it represented.

War and plague had helped to undermine 'ancestral values', social no less than religious. The hominocentric bias of the fifth-century intellectual movement (summed up by Protagoras' famous dictum that 'Man is the measure of all things') both exposed the hollowness of Olympianism – always an 'established', *i.e.* predominantly upper-class, cult – and at the same time proved wholly inadequate, through its very nature, to provide an acceptable *emotional* substitute. Hence the superstitions, magic, astrology and 'enthusiastic' cults (mostly of foreign origin) which from now on steadily gained ground in the Greek-speaking world. Hence, too, the increasing, and essentially pessimistic, tendency to see life in terms of Chance, as a kind of vast and impersonal roulette-wheel. Hence, in the last resort, what we label the 'romantic element' in later Greek art and literature: the emphasis on individual (and often morbid) psychology, the inclination to value sensibility above reason – all uncannily foreshadowed by Euripides, a writer half a century ahead of his time.

One striking contrast between the literature of the Periclean era and that of the fourth century is the latter's increasing emphasis (though

201 Votive relief from Delos (the Agora of the Italians, first century BC), offered to Isis Pelagia ('of the Sea').

still slight by our standards) on business affairs, economics and finance. This, like the concern with private rather than public litigation, is just what we might expect from the general climate of opinion. So, indeed, are the contrasting philosophical attitudes of Socrates' two immediate successors, Aristippus and Antisthenes, who between them sum up a polarization of beliefs that was to persist throughout the Hellenistic era into Graeco-Roman and Christian times. Aristippus of Cyrene (a luxury-loving character who at one time was a courtier under Dionysius I, the tyrant of Syracuse) held – a view more fully formulated by his grandson of the same name – that immediate pleasure was the only end of action, that knowledge was sensation, the here-and-now the one true reality. Antisthenes, his diametrical opposite in every sense, rejected the pleasure principle as madness, advocating instead an austere way of life based on thrift, poverty, independence of mind, and – a significant new feature – contempt for the world and its affairs.

Fifty years earlier, such isolationism would have been almost unthinkable as a way of life. It is possible that the final phases of the war, and the political crises which followed, did much to alienate men of a naturally ascetic or authoritarian temperament. Such persons – a

202 Attis and Cybele in front of the goddess's temple, on a votive relief from Asia Minor (second century BC). Cybele stands on the left, flanked by a lion, wearing a mural crown and carrying a patera (dish). Attis is in the centre in a frontal pose.

Plato no less than an Antisthenes – must have viewed the world around them with ever-increasing disgust, and have sought fervently (the leitmotiv appears again and again from now on) for some stable unchanging permanence behind the flux and chaos of appearances. These were the conditions which bred, not only the Platonic Theory of Ideas, but also a preoccupation with what we now term Utopias – theoretical blueprints for a new and better society. Of these by far the most famous is the polity adumbrated by Plato in his *Republic* (a misleading if traditional title: *Society* or *The State* would be more accurate), which he probably wrote between 386, the foundation-year of the Academy, and 380.

To read the *Republic* after half a century of totalitarian upheaval in Europe and elsewhere can be a bleakly unnerving experience. Plato's ideal rule by 'Guardians' (a notion adopted, with some enthusiasm, by the Nazi Party) embodies nearly all the more objectionable practices of both fascism and communism, with a little Inquisition fire-and-faggotry thrown in for good measure. In historical terms, such a development was all too predictable. Plato had lived through the purges carried out by the Thirty Tyrants only to watch, with equal horror, as the restored democracy condemned his friend and master Socrates. For him, all existing political groups had proved themselves bankrupt. From this premiss it was only a short step to the belief that political *areté* could be achieved through moral self-examination alone, and that political leadership must be made conditional on the most rigorous intellectual, ethical and moral training. His rejection of the democratic process (which he rated only one degree better than tyranny) was total. What he offered instead was intellectual elitism dispensed by a group of authoritarian paternalists, themselves trained under a 'philosopher-king'.

Despite this revolutionary programme, Plato was, paradoxically, still enough of an Athenian traditionalist to retain a fundamental belief in the *polis* (as Aristotle did after him), and to make his ideal citizens, even more than fifth-century practice would have prescribed, mere specialized functionaries, extensions of the city's collective existence and will. Yet in the last resort it was his own class background which predisposed him towards authoritarianism, legislation *de haut en bas* by a cultured aristocrat for the benefit of the faceless multitude. The increasing irresponsibility demonstrated by the Athenian *demos* during Plato's lifetime merely served to make his theories sound all too plausible. In such a climate, it is small wonder that many intelligent citizens seriously turned back to the old idea of a 'strong man' solution. By an odd turn of fate, both the man and the moment were at hand. Monarchy, long abandoned as a primitive anachronism, was due for a remarkable new lease of life.

Philip and the Greeks

Philip II of Macedonia, who ascended the throne when his brother
Perdiccas died in battle against the Illyrians (359), ruled over an area,
and a people, commonly regarded by city-state intellectuals as no less
'barbarous' than Thrace – and as negligible politically. Despite their
sub-Homeric culture, Macedonia's warriors had not shown to any
great advantage on the battlefield. Their uncouth drinking habits and
murderous dynastic intrigues were regarded with patronizing
contempt, as mere tribal antics. Macedonia, like Scotland, is divided
into lowlands and highlands, with a great double horseshoe of hills
and mountains enclosing the fertile plain above the Thermaic Gulf.
The wild clans of the highlands had, since time immemorial, been
ruled over by their own princes. Since the early fifth century, however,
the lowland dynasty of the Argeads, with its capital first at Aegae and,
latterly, down in the plain at Pella, had held at least titular sway over
Macedonia as a whole. Its record hitherto had been colourful rather
than impressive.

Alexander I steered Macedonia through the Persian Wars by
collaborating with both sides as occasion dictated. Perdiccas II spent
much of the Peloponnesian War switching his allegiance, with
dizzying rapidity, and selling shipbuilding lumber simultaneously to
Athens and her opponents, like some primitive armaments con-
sortium. Archelaus I (413–399) tried his hand at a little Hellenization,
luring such star attractions as Euripides to his court to provide

203 The Macedonian Royal
Palace, Pella: note the
chequered pebble-mosaic floor-
ing. Excavations in Philip's
and Alexander's capital have
revealed a degree of affluence
and taste that does much to
counter contemporary Greek
charges of Macedonian 'bar-
barism'.

204, 205 Top: obverse of Macedonian stater minted by Archelaus I (413–399 BC). Above: obverse of Macedonian stater minted by Amyntas III (393–370 BC), portraying a bearded Heracles wearing a lionskin. It is possible that both these coins, with their sharply distinguished heads, portray the reigning monarch.

206 Below: bronze arrowhead found at Olynthus, inscribed with Philip's name, and clearly datable to the siege of 348 BC. Earlier, in 354, Philip had had one eye shot out by an archer with a similarly inscribed arrow, and the Olynthians were clearly trying to repeat this success.

cultural uplift. The old-guard Macedonian barons, who much preferred hunting, drinking and debauchery, were not impressed. In the forty-odd years following Archelaus' death Macedonia had seven or eight rulers, few of whom died in their beds: the period is characterized by constant encroachments from abroad, combined with Borgia-like intrigue at home. Amyntas III (393–370) lasted longer than most. However, his chief legacy to Macedonia was a trio of sons – Alexander, Perdiccas, Philip – sired in his old age.

The first two died young, one assassinated, the other, as we have seen, in battle – though not before they had done a good deal to strengthen and stabilize the Macedonian army, especially by the establishment of an elite infantry corps, the so-called 'Foot Companions' (*pezetairoi*). Perdiccas III's massive defeat by the Illyrians was a major setback: four thousand men, the King himself included, were left dead on the battlefield. Philip could not have taken over in less propitious circumstances. Yet within twenty years he had made his country the most powerful state in the entire Balkan peninsula, thereby radically transforming the balance of power throughout the Greek world. With his reign, and that of his more famous son Alexander, Greek history enters on a completely new phase.

What Philip saw, very clearly, was that Macedonia's centralized, autocratic system of government could prove immensely advantageous – especially against ill-co-ordinated, quarrelsome, anarchic democracies – if exploited to the full by a strong, ambitious ruler. Having disposed of all potential rivals to the throne in very short order, Philip set about strengthening his frontiers and acquiring fresh territory, by that idiosyncratic mixture of military force, diplomatic double-talk and psychological acumen which formed his special, never-to-be-repeated brand of international power politics. By 349 he had worked out a complex expansionist policy which was beginning to cause great alarm among the Greek states. He now (349–346) set about the reduction of the Chalcidic peninsula. While the fate of its capital, Olynthus, hung in the balance, the Athenian orator Demosthenes – like Churchill in the 1930s – called imperiously for firm action before it was too late.

His fellow countrymen, while admiring Demosthenes' impassioned oratory, failed to agree – till it was too late – on sending an expeditionary force to relieve the beleaguered city. Olynthus fell to Philip in 348, and two years later (after he had mopped up some thirty further towns around the Chalcidic peninsula) Athens decided to negotiate a peace treaty with him. Philip stalled the ambassadors, played them off against each other, and finally gave them a concordat, the so-called 'Peace of Philocrates' (346: named after the leader of the Athenian delegation) which did little more than endorse the *status quo*, including all Philip's new territorial acquisitions. Not all Demosthenes' contemporaries believed in last-ditch resistance as a solution, either (again, parallels from the 1930s suggest themselves). As early as 355 that veteran political pundit Isocrates was urging Athens to give up all idea of a maritime empire, and later advised her to join a Panhellenic League against Persia – under Philip's leadership.

The Macedonian King was expert at lulling unwelcome suspicions; but foreign observers, one feels, might have taken more account of his extensive and remarkable army reforms. A man who creates a professional as opposed to a conscript army, trains it constantly, and keeps it mobilized on a permanent rather than a seasonal basis, may be presumed to have a good practical reason for so doing. Philip expanded the old Foot Companions into a formidable heavy-infantry phalanx: sixteen ranks deep rather than the normal eight, and far more flexible, its members equipped with light-weight armour and the terrible Macedonian pike (*sarissa*), some twelve to thirteen feet in length. He also built up a corps of elite shock-troops, the Guards Brigade (*hypaspistae*). Most of these innovations Philip had learnt from the great Epaminondas in Thebes, where he had spent several years of his adolescence as a highly observant hostage.

However, Philip's most characteristic battle strategy (subsequently borrowed by Alexander at the Granicus and Issus) seems to have been his own invention. This was the echeloned or slantwise attack, in which left and centre were deliberately held back ('refused') while the right engaged – a movement always liable to stretch the enemy line. Into the resultant thinning, or gap, a living wedge, the Companion Cavalry, would charge, from the right flank, leaving the infantry to follow and consolidate. Philip employed this device, with striking success, in his first major battle against the Illyrians (359), and again at Chaeronea in 338 – though on this latter occasion it was the *left* wing, under his eighteen-year-old son Alexander, that delivered the *coup de grâce*. Unlike most first-class army commanders, however, Philip was also a seasoned and subtle politician, prouder of the victories he scored through diplomacy than those he won on the field of battle.

Year after year, while Philip steadily built up his position, Athens remained hamstrung by violent party in-fighting on foreign policy, collaboration versus appeasement – a division sedulously fostered by Philip himself. In autumn 344 Demosthenes delivered his famous Second Philippic, the gist of which was that, despite his flowery protestations, Philip would never rest until he had brought Athens to her knees – in part by the conscious exploitation of Athenian longing for peace. A so-called 'Sacred War' over the control of Delphi gave Philip the excuse to move his forces down into central Greece. This

207 Roman copy of the statue of Demosthenes by Polyeuktos, erected at the request of Demosthenes' nephew Demochares, forty-two years after his death (i.e. in 280 BC), and set up in the Athenian Agora, near the Altar of the Twelve Gods.

news caused real panic at Athens and Thebes, so much so that, despite their long-standing hostility, they hastily patched up an anti-Macedonian alliance. On 2 August 338 Philip came through the Boeotian passes, and two days later brought the Greeks to battle at Chaeronea. His victory was total and momentous: all organized resistance to Macedonia now ceased. Chaeronea spelt the end of city-state freedom as any *polis*-based democrat understood it. The 'strong man' solution had been applied at last.

Aristotle, who had ties with both Macedonia and Athens (as tutor to the young Alexander, and first head of that remarkable college-cum-research centre, the Lyceum) must have greeted the news with mixed feelings. Yet in the last resort the entire intellectual climate which he and Plato had helped to evolve was – disclaimers notwithstanding – well in key with this new authoritarianism. Aristotle's engrained class prejudices and contempt for 'lesser breeds' (not to

208 The marble 'Lion of Chaeronea', set on a plinth to commemorate, and guard, the common tomb in which members of the Theban Sacred Band were buried after Philip's victory (338 BC). Excavation of the tomb brought to light 254 skeletons, laid out in seven rows.

mention all manual labour: could gentlemen, he asked, properly play musical instruments?), his intellectual elitism and meritocratic pretensions, his fascination with monarchy and absolute power – such phenomena leave one (as no doubt they left many Greeks) nursing a sense of profound depression. It is as though the previous two centuries, from Solon to Pericles and the great Attic dramatists, had been lived in vain. Intellect, now, had entered the service of absolutism, with which it had always had a social, class-based sympathy. Aristotle may refer only in passing to Philip or Alexander in the *Politics*, but their great shadows lie across every page: the kings of surpassing *areté* before whom all must bow down and worship, the strong men whose sharply dictatorial swords slashed through the more-than-Gordian knot of fourth-century Greek politics, the shattered coda of what, for all its faults, had been the most exciting and progressive political movement yet known to mankind.

Alexander the Great: a myth and an enigma

After his victory at Chaeronea, Philip of Macedon sent ambassadors to Athens with generous terms for a peace settlement: more generous by far than those he offered Thebes. As one of his representatives (and escorts for the ashes of the Athenian dead, now returned home with honour), he chose his own son, Alexander, now eighteen (b. 356). This remarkable young man – blond, stocky, quick-witted, a fast runner and born horseman – had been carefully trained as Philip's successor since childhood. His tutors and educational programme were carefully chosen with this end in view. His terrible mother, Olympias, taught him to think of himself as a king, and perhaps something more than a king: it may well have been she who infected him, at an impressionable age, with notions of his own divinity.

Ambition is a virus easily caught, and Alexander was no more immune to it than the next man. He embraced the Homeric code of the Argeads with enthusiasm, grafting on to it a personal sense of identification with Achilles. That hero's touchy pride and thirst for military glory, his determination 'ever to be best and above all others', are traits which at once strike us in Philip's son. From the tutelage of Aristotle he acquired, not only a lifelong interest in medicine and botany, but also a sense of his own kingly *areté*, and a traditional contempt (which expediency and experience soon made him modify) for all non-Hellenes. There is a famous fragment of Aristotle's in which he advises Alexander to be 'a leader to the Greeks and a despot to the barbarians, to look after the former as after friends and relatives, and to deal with the latter as with beasts or plants'. In this attitude he had the backing of almost all Greek intellectuals, Euripides and Plato included.

209 Marble head of Alexander the Great from Pergamum; probably contemporary with the great altar built by Eumenes II (197–159 BC). The characteristic lion's-mane hair and tilted head may possibly derive from earlier statues by Lysippus, the King's official portrait-sculptor.

Though Alexander seems to have discarded such a notion later (even this has been disputed) he surely embraced it with some enthusiasm as a young man. To invade the Persian Empire offered an unparalleled opportunity for the achievement of military *areté*; besides, he had been brought up to regard this crusade as his natural heritage. His future, in that autumn of 338, looked bright with promise. Yet there were already tensions below the surface. How long would Alexander remain content with the status of Crown Prince now plans for the great invasion were actually under way? Kingship was Alexander's destiny, the legitimate conquest of Persia his birthright. Yet between him and this glittering prospect there stood one formidable obstacle: his father. Philip was now in his mid-forties, battle-scarred and battered by hard living, yet still as full of energy and ambition as ever.

Unless some chance arrow struck him down – and he seemed to bear a charmed life – it was Philip, not his son, who would earn immortality as the conqueror of the Persian Empire. As time went on, this realization clearly caused acute friction between father and son. It may have had more serious consequences still. Rightly or wrongly,

Philip came to suspect Alexander and Olympias of plotting a coup against him. This is the only possible explanation of his behaviour between 338 and 336. He first (in striking contrast to his earlier policy) eased Alexander out of all public functions. He then proceeded to divorce Olympias on the ground of adultery (at the same time casting doubts on Alexander's parentage), and, finally, married as his fifth wife a blue-blooded Macedonian aristocrat, whose uncle prayed at the wedding-feast that from this union might spring a *legitimate heir* to the Argead throne. If Philip, that canny diplomat, was prepared to ditch his well-trained Crown Prince in so public and humiliating a fashion, it could only be because he feared him as a potential rival and usurper.

Philip's first child by his new wife was a girl, which may explain why he now, surprisingly, patched up a reconciliation with his angry son. With the Persian venture imminent, even a suspect Crown Prince was better than none. An advance force had already set out, to establish a bridgehead at the Hellespont crossing, and, as Philip put it, to 'liberate the Greek cities'. The Delphic Oracle, on being asked whether Philip would conquer the Great King, replied, ambiguously: 'The bull is garlanded. All is done. The sacrifice is ready.' To secure his western frontier, finally, Philip arranged a marriage between Olympias' brother, Alexander of Epirus, and her daughter Cleopatra, Alexander's sister. Incest, clearly, was no impediment to a good alliance. The wedding took place at the old Macedonian capital of Aegae – shortly after Philip's wife gave birth to a son – and ambassadors and notables from every Greek city were invited to attend it. On the second day of the festivities, in circumstances which have never been fully cleared up, Philip was assassinated by a member of his own bodyguard. The garlanded bull had indeed been sacrificed – but at whose instigation?

Circumstantial evidence, then as now, pointed ineluctably to Alexander and Olympias. Proof positive is out of the question; it can only be said that Philip's death was little short of providential for his son. With swift assurance Alexander won the army's endorsement as King, secured recognition from those foreign envoys so conveniently assembled in Aegae, and almost at once set out on that career of conquest which has earned him an immortal if ambivalent niche in history. After one swift campaign (335) to subdue recalcitrant frontier tribesmen and cow potentially rebellious Greek states – including the utter destruction of Thebes, a piece of calculated terrorism which misfired rather badly – Alexander crossed into Asia Minor (spring 334), leaving Antipater behind as Regent, with a strong home army to keep the Balkans in order. He was never to set foot on Macedonian soil again.

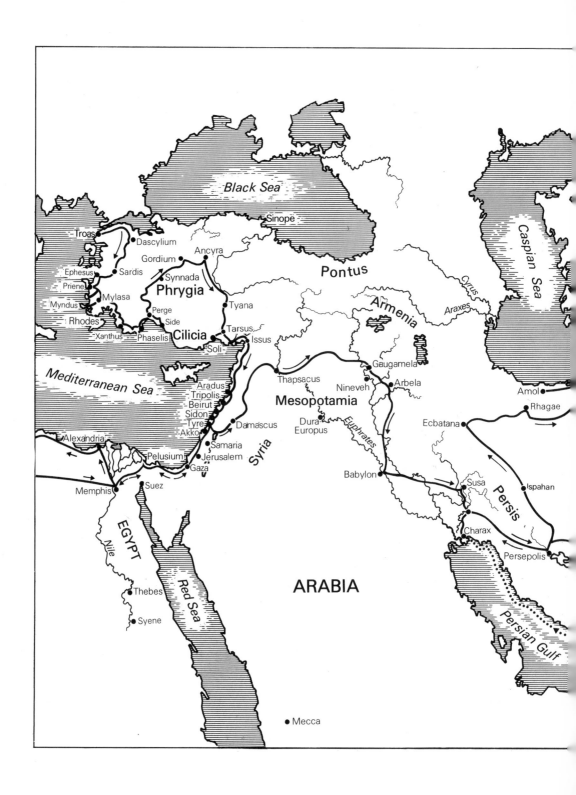

Map scale:
0 — 250 — 500 Mls
0 — 400 — 800 Kms

Aral Sea

Oxus

Tashkent

Cyropolis

Bokhara • Marakanda

Karshi • Derbent

Bactria

~Bujnurd

• Meshed

rthia

Aria

Artacoana •

Alexandria Areion

Kabul

Bucephala Alexandria

Taxila

Sialcot

Desert

Drangiana

Arachosia

• Farah

Kandahar •

• Nad-i-Ali

• Quetta

Indus

INDIA

• Salmous (Gulashkird)

• Harmozia

Gedrosia

• Lus Bela

Gwadur Pasni

Kokala

Nearchus' voyage

Oman

Indian Ocean

210 Map of the route of Alexander's conquests: the King's
route covered over twenty
thousand miles in all, from
Macedonia to what is now
West Pakistan, and back as
far as Babylon. His hold on
India was precarious, and soon
lost after his death; but the
great Persian Empire was par-
celled out among his marshals,
changing the whole shape of
the Mediterranean and Near
East world for centuries.

169

211 Right: the so-called 'Chigi relief' commemorating the Battle of Gaugamela: carved plaque of yellow marble, dating from the reign of the Emperor Tiberius (42 BC–AD 37).

212, 213 Opposite, above: Alexander's conquests spread cultural and social influences throughout the Near and Middle East. Detail of a fresco from a decorated tomb, at Marissa in Idumaea (third century BC) showing a Macedonian with a pike, with which he is killing a leopard already wounded by a dart. The hunter is accompanied by a trumpeter and two dogs. Below: obverse of a gold medallion showing Alexander, from Abukir (first half of second century BC).

His march of conquest – if not to the world's end, at least beyond the limits of Darius I's empire at its most extensive – was a legendary achievement in military terms, though his motives for undertaking it have been much romanticized. His vision of world conquest, it is safe to say, did not spring from any grandiose feeling for the Brotherhood of Man. His policy of racial fusion between Greeks and Orientals, like his adaptation of Persian court protocol, stemmed in the first instance from practical administrative needs. But his sheer record of conquest was stunning enough in itself. Three brilliantly fought major battles – the Granicus (334), Issus (333) and Gaugamela (331) – shattered the Achaemenid Empire and left Alexander himself *de facto* Lord of Asia. His eastward quest for Ocean was halted only by faulty geographical knowledge and a full-dress mutiny by his exhausted veterans. When he died in Babylon (June 323), perhaps of malaria, more probably by poison, he was busy planning fresh campaigns in

Arabia and the west. By then he had also, arguably, become insane, a classic case of alcoholic megalomania. His demand to be worshipped as a god was only one symptom of this condition.

Whatever our assessment of Alexander the man, there can be no doubt as to his immense impact on the whole Greek-speaking world. He flooded the Mediterranean with gold bullion 'liberated' from Susa and Persepolis, an act which caused serious economic problems for his successors. Though he was not, as has sometimes been alleged, the first ruler to open up regular trade-routes between east and west, he certainly promoted the extensive Hellenization of an area stretching far beyond the Hindu Kush. The scientists and surveyors who accompanied his expedition laid the foundations of all future classical knowledge concerning eastern geography, and brought home a wealth of data relating to the flora, fauna, mineral resources and social *mores* of the exotic countries through which they passed. Greek

dynasties in regions as remote as Bactria brought Hellenic government, ideas, even sculptural iconography to alien cultures one might have thought wholly immune to such influences. In more ways than one, Alexander changed the shape of the known world, besides bringing much that had hitherto been unknown within the compass of contemporary civilization.

He also set up the pattern for a new age. Though the vast empire he carved out fell apart almost immediately after his death, its *disiecta membra* – bitterly fought over for forty years and more by his surviving senior officers – formed the basis for those great 'Successor Kingdoms' which dominated the Greek-speaking world until their final absorption by Rome. His insistence on deification set a popular trend in emperor-worship which led directly to figures such as Antiochus Epiphanes and, later, Elagabalus. The myth and enigma of his personality far outstripped its merely historical context, becoming in later centuries a touchstone for every kind of idealized exploration and romantic striving after eternal glory. Classical Greece died with Alexander: indeed, it might be said to have died at Chaeronea. What followed – that many-faceted, brilliant phenomenon known to scholars as the Hellenistic Age – ushers in a new chapter of European history.

Select Bibliography

Note: This bibliography is specifically designed to help non-specialist readers who want more detailed information concerning the various topics touched on in this brief survey. It does not, therefore, include any foreign works, or (with one important exception) articles in specialist periodicals, or studies which require knowledge of ancient Greek, e.g. Meiggs and Lewis's indispensable *Greek Historical Inscriptions*. It does, on the other hand, list the main primary sources for the period in translation. To avoid excessive cross-indexing, titles are listed alphabetically according to author; the descriptive rubric in the left-hand column offers a quick guide to subject-matter. Works of especial interest or value are marked with a star, thus:*.

Text	ADAMS, C.D. *The Speeches of Aeschines*. London (Loeb) 1919.
Historiography	ADCOCK, F.E. *Thucydides and his History*. Cambridge U.P. 1963.
Social Studies	ADKINS, A.W.H. *Merit and responsibility: a study in Greek values*. Oxford 1960.*
Social Studies	— *From the Many to the One: a study of personality and views of human nature in the context of ancient Greek societies, values and beliefs*. Cornell 1970.
Social Studies	— *Moral values and political behaviour in Ancient Greece*. London 1972.*
Crete	ALEXIOU, S., PLATON, N., GUANELLA, H., MATT, L. VON. *Ancient Crete*. London 1968.*
Philosophy	ALLAN, D.J. *The philosophy of Aristotle*. London 1952.
Economics	ANDREADES, A.M. *A History of Greek Public Finance*. Vol. I, rev. ed. Cambridge 1933.
Political	ANDREWES, A. *The Greek Tyrants*. London 1956.
	— *The Greeks*. London 1967.
Topographical	ANDREWS, K. *Athens* [Cities of the World, No. 7]. London 1967.*
Art	ARIAS, P.E., HIRMER, M. *A History of Greek Vase Painting*. London 1962.
Political	BARKER, E. *Greek Political Theory*. 5th ed. London 1960.
Bronze Age	BARNETT, R.D. *The Sea Peoples*. Cambridge U.P. 1969 [= CAH³ Vol. II, Ch. 28].
Text	BARNSTONE, W. *Greek Lyric Poetry*. Indiana 1962.
Architecture	BERVE, H., GRUBEN, G., HIRMER, M. *Greek Temples, Theatres and Shrines*. London 1963 (o.p.).
Troy	BLEGEN, C.W. *Troy*. Cambridge U.P. 1964 [= CAH³ Vol. I, sections from Chs 18, 24; Vol. II, sections from Chs 15, 21].

Troy	BLEGEN, C.W. *Troy and the Trojans*. New York 1963.
Art	BOARDMAN, J. *Greek Art*. London and New York 1964.
Colonization	– *The Greeks Overseas*. Harmondsworth 1964.
Art/Architecture	– (with DÖRIG, J., FUCHS, W., HIRMER, M.) *The Art and Architecture of Ancient Greece*. London 1967.
Social	BONNER, R.J., SMITH, G. *The administration of justice from Homer to Aristotle*. 2 vols. Chicago 1930.
Text	BOWERSOCK, G.W. Xenophon, Scripta Minora, pp. 474 ff. [*The Constitution of the Athenians.*] London (Loeb) 1968.
Literature	BOWRA, C.M. *Greek Lyric Poetry*. 2nd ed. Oxford 1961.
Literature	– *Early Greek Elegists*. Harvard U.P. 1938.
Text	– *The Odes of Pindar*. Harmondsworth 1969.
Athens, 5th C.	– *Periclean Athens*. London 1971.
Literature	– *Pindar*. Oxford 1964.*
Philosophy	BRÉHIER, E. *The history of philosophy: the Hellenic age*. Trs. J. Thomas. Chicago 1963.
Alexander	BURN, A.R. *Alexander the Great and the Hellenistic World*. Rev. ed. New York 1962.
Archaic Age	– *The Lyric Age of Greece*. London 1960.*
General	– *The Pelican History of Greece*. Harmondsworth 1966.
Athens, 5th C.	– *Pericles and Athens*. New York 1949.
Persian Wars	– *Persia and the Greeks*. London 1962.*
Text	BURTT, J.O. *Minor Attic Orators*. Vol. II. London (Loeb) 1954.
General	BURY, J.B. *A History of Greece to the death of Alexander the Great*. 3rd ed. rev. Russell Meiggs. London 1967.
Prehistory	*Cambridge Ancient History*. Vol. I, Pt. i, 'Prolegomena and Prehistory'. 3rd ed. Cambridge U.P. 1970.*
Prehistory	– Vol. I, Pt. ii, 'Early History of the Middle East'. 3rd ed. Cambridge U.P. 1971.
Prehistory	– Vol. II, Pt. i, 'The Middle East and the Aegean Region, *c.* 1800–1380 BC. Cambridge U.P. 1973.
4th cent.	– Vol. VI, 'Macedon 401–301 BC'. Cambridge U.P. 1953.
Dark Ages	CARPENTER, R. *Discontinuity in Greek Civilisation*. C.U.P. 1966.
Historiography	CARY, M. *The documentary sources of Greek history*. Oxford 1927.
Historiography	– *The geographic background of Greek and Roman history*. Oxford 1949.
Bronze Age	CASKEY, J.L. *Greece, Crete, and the Aegean Islands in the Early* Cambridge U.P. 1966 [*CAH³ Vol. I, Chs 9(c), 26(b); Vol. II, Chs 4(c) 22(b)].
Bronze Age	– *Greece and the Aegean Islands in the Middle Bronze Age*. Cambridge U.P. 1966 [= CAH³ Vol. II, Ch. 4(a)].
Bronze Age	CATLING, H.W. *Cyprus in the Neolithic and Bronze Age periods*. Cambridge U.P. 1966 [= CAH³ Vol. I, Chs 9(c), 26(b); Vol. II, Chs 4(c), 22 (b)].
Linguistics	CHADWICK, J. *The Prehistory of the Greek Language*. Cambridge U.P. 1963 [= CAH³ Vol. II, Ch. 39].
Linguistics	– *The Decipherment of Linear B*. 2nd ed. Cambridge U.P. 1962.
Medicine/Text	– (with MANN, W.N.) *The Medical Works of Hippocrates*. Oxford 1950.
Art	CHARBONNEAUX, J., MARTIN, R., VILLARD, F. *Archaic Greek Art, 620–480 BC*. Trs. James Emmons and Robert Allen. London 1971.*

Art	– *Classical Greek Art, 480–330 B C.* London 1973.
Sparta	CHRIMES, K.M.T. *Ancient Sparta.* London 1949.
Science	CLAGETT, M. *Greek Science in Antiquity.* London 1957.
Historiography	COCHRANE, C.N. *Thucydides and the Science of History.* Oxford 1929.
Science	COHEN, M.R., DRABKIN, I.E. *A Source Book in Greek Science.* Harvard U.P. 1958.*
Colonization	COOK, J.M. *The Greeks in Ionia and the East.* London 1962.
Colonization	– *Greek settlement in the Eastern Aegean and Asia Minor.* Cambridge U.P. 1961 [=CAH³ Vol. II, Ch. 38].
Art	COOK, R.M. *Greek Painted Pottery.* London 1960.*
General	– *The Greeks until Alexander.* London/New York 1962.
Philosophy	CORNFORD, F.M. *From Religion to Philosophy. A study in the origins of Western speculation.* London 1912.
Philosophy	– *Before and After Socrates.* Cambridge 1932.
Historiography	– *Thucydides Mythistoricus.* London 1907; repr. New York 1969.
Prehistory	CROSSLAND, R.A. *Immigrants from the North.* Cambridge U.P. 1967 [=CAH³ Vol. I, Ch. 27].
Persia	CULICAN, W. *The Medes and Persians.* London 1965.
Text	DAVENPORT, G. *Carmina Archilochi: The Fragments of Archilochos.* Univ. of California Press 1964.
Dark Ages	DESBOROUGH, V.R.d'A. *The last Mycenaeans and their successors.* Oxford 1964.
Dark Ages	– *The Greek Dark Ages.* London 1972.
Dark Ages	– (and HAMMOND, N.G.L.) *The end of Mycenaean Civilisation and the Dark Age.* Cambridge U.P. 1962 [=CAH³ Vol. II, Ch. 36].
Text	DICKINSON, P. *Aristophanes, Plays I and II.* 2 vols. Oxford U.P. 1970.
Architecture	DINSMOOR, W.B. *The architecture of ancient Greece.* 3rd ed. London 1950.
Social Studies	DODDS, E.R. *The Greeks and the Irrational.* Berkeley 1951.*
Literature	DOVER, K.J. *Aristophanic Comedy.* London 1972.
Medicine	EDELSTEIN, L. *Ancient medicine.* Baltimore (John Hopkins) 1967.
Alexander	EHRENBERG, V. *Alexander and the Greeks.* Oxford 1938.
General	– *From Solon to Socrates: Greek history and civilisation during the sixth and fifth centuries B C.* London 1968.
Political	– *The Greek State.* Oxford 1960.
Social Studies	– *The people of Aristophanes.* 2nd ed. Oxford 1951.
Athens, 5th C.	– *Sophocles and Pericles.* Oxford 1954.
Text	EVELYN-WHITE, H.G. *Hesiod, the Homeric Hymns, and Homerica.* Rev. ed. London (Loeb) 1936.
Science	FARRINGTON, B. *Greek science.* Harmondsworth 1961.
Literature	FINLEY, J.H. *Pindar and Aeschylus.* Harvard U.P. 1955.
Historiography	– *Thucydides.* 2nd ed. Michigan 1947.
Historiography	– *Three essays on Thucydides.* Harvard U.P. 1967.
General	FINLEY, M.I. *The Ancient Greeks.* London 1963.
Bronze Age	– *Early Greece: the Bronze and Archaic Ages.* London 1970.
Dark Ages	– *The World of Odysseus.* London 1956.*
Sicily	– *A History of Sicily. Vol. I: Ancient Sicily.* London 1968.
Political	– *The Ancestral Constitution.* Cambridge 1971.

Social Studies	FLACELIÈRE, R. *Daily life in Greece at the time of Pericles.* Trs. P. Green. London 1965.
Historiography	FORNARA, C.W. *Herodotus: an interpretative essay.* Oxford 1971.
Political	FORREST, W.G. *The emergence of Greek democracy: the character of Greek politics, 800–400 B C.* London 1966.*
Sparta	– *A History of Sparta, 950–192 B C.* London 1968.
Philosophy	FREEMAN, K. *Ancilla to the Presocratic Philosophers.* Oxford 1948.
Political	– *Life and work of Solon.* London 1926.
Economics	FRENCH, A. *The growth of the Athenian economy.* London 1964.*
Philosophy	FRIEDLÄNDER, P. *Plato: an introduction.* Trs. H. Meyerhoff. Rev. ed. Princeton U.P. 1970.
Political/Text	FRITZ, K. VON, KAPP, E. *Aristotle's 'Constitution of Athens' and related texts.* New York 1950.
General	FROST, F.J. *Greek Society.* Lexington, Mass. 1971.
Persia	FRYE, R.N. *The heritage of Persia.* London 1963.
Alexander	FULLER, J.F.C. *The Generalship of Alexander the Great.* London 1958.
Persia	GHIRSHMAN, R. *Persia: from the origins to Alexander the Great.* Trs. S. Gilbert and J. Emmons. London 1964.
Political	GLOTZ, G. *The Greek City and its Institutions.* London 1929.
Colonization	GRAHAM, A.J. *Colony and Mother City in Ancient Greece.* New York 1964.
Crete	GRAHAM, J.W. *The Palaces of Crete.* Princeton 1962.
Alexander	GREEN, P. *Alexander the Great.* London 1970.
Sicily/Athens	– *Armada from Athens: the failure of the Sicilian Expedition, 415–413 B C.* London 1971.
Persian Wars	– *The Year of Salamis: 480–479 B C.* London 1970.
Text	GRENE, D., LATTIMORE, R. (ed.). *The Complete Greek Tragedies.* Chicago, various dates.
General	GROTE, G. *A History of Greece.* New ed., 10 vols. London 1888.
Philosophy	GRUBE, G.M.A. *Plato's Thought.* London 1935.
Historiography	GRUNDY, G.B. *Thucydides and the History of his Age.* 2nd ed. Oxford 1948.
Religion	GUTHRIE, W.K.C. *The Greeks and their Gods.* London 1950.
Philosophy	– *In the Beginning.* London 1957.
Philosophy	– *A History of Greek Philosophy.* Vol. I, *The Earlier Presocratics and the Pythagoreans* (1962); Vol. II, *The Presocratic Tradition from Parmenides to Democritus* (1965); Vol. III, *The Fifth-Century Enlightenment* (1969),* all Cambridge U.P.
General	HAMMOND, N.G.L. *A History of Greece to 322 B C.* 2nd ed. Oxford 1967.
Reference	– (with SCULLARD, H.H.) *The Oxford Classical Dictionary.* 2nd ed. Oxford 1970.
Literature	HARRISON, E. *Studies in Theognis.* Cambridge U.P. 1902.
Economics	HASEBROEK, J. *Trade and Politics in ancient Greece.* Trs. L.M. Fraser and D.C. MacGregor. London 1933.
General	HATZFELD, J. *History of Ancient Greece.* Rev. A. Aymard, trs. A.C. Harrison, ed. E.H. Goddard. London 1966.
Political	HAVELOCK, E.A. *The Liberal Temper in Greek Politics.* London 1957.
Science	HEATH, T.L. *Greek Astronomy.* London 1932.
Science	– *A History of Greek Mathematics.* Vol. I, Oxford 1921.

Medicine	HEIDEL, W.A. *Hippocratic medicine: its spirit and method.* New York 1941.
Religion/Athens	HERINGTON, C.J. *Athena Parthenos and Athena Polias: a study in the religion of Periclean Athens.* Manchester U.P. 1955.*
Art	HIGGINS, R.A. *Greek and Roman Jewellery.* London 1962.
Art	– *Minoan and Mycenaean Art.* London and New York 1967.
Political	HIGNETT, C. *A History of the Athenian Constitution to the end of the fifth century BC.* Oxford 1952.
Persian Wars	– *Xerxes' Invasion of Greece.* Oxford 1963.
Topographical/ Athens	HILL, I.T. *The ancient city of Athens: its topography and monuments.* London 1953; repr. Chicago 1969.
Prehistory	HOOD, S. *The home of the heroes: the Aegean before the Greeks.* London 1967.
Art/Architecture	HOOKER, G.T.W. (ed.) *Parthenos and Parthenon* [*Greece and Rome,* Suppl. to Vol. x]. Oxford 1963.
Topographical/ Athens	HOPPER, R.J. *The Acropolis.* London 1971.
Crete	HUTCHINSON, R.W. *Prehistoric Crete.* Harmondsworth 1962.
Colonization	HUXLEY, G.L. *The early Ionians.* London 1966.
Philosophy	JAEGER, W. *Aristotle.* Trs. R. Robinson. 2nd ed. Oxford 1948.
Political	JONES, A.H.M. *Athenian Democracy.* Oxford 1957.
Sparta	– *Sparta.* Oxford 1967.
Medicine	JONES, W.H.S. *Philosophy and medicine in ancient Greece.* Baltimore (Johns Hopkins) 1946.
Medicine/Text	– (with WITHINGTON, E.T.) *Hippocrates.* 4 vols. London (Loeb) 1923–31.
Athens, 5th C.	KAGAN, D. *The outbreak of the Peloponnesian War.* Cornell 1969.
Reference	KIEPERT, H. *Atlas antiquus.* Berlin 1890.
Philosophy	KIRK, G.S. *Heraclitus, the Cosmic Fragments.* Cambridge U.P. 1954.
Literature/ Historiography	– *The Homeric poems as history.* Cambridge U.P. 1964 [= CAH³ Vol. II, Ch. 39(b)].
Bronze Age	– (ed.) *The language and background of Homer.* Cambridge 1964 [see esp. DOW, S. 'The Greeks in the Bronze Age', pp. 140–173].
Philosophy	– (and RAVEN, J.E.) *The Presocratic Philosophers.* Cambridge U.P. 1957.
General	KITTO, H.D.F. *The Greeks.* Harmondsworth (rev. ed.) 1957.
Numismatics	KRAAY, C.M., HIRMER, M. *Greek Coins.* London/New York 1966.
Social Studies	KURTZ, D.C., BOARDMAN, J. *Greek Burial Customs.* London 1971.
Social Studies	LACEY, W.K. *The Family in Classical Greece.* London and Cornell 1968.
General	LAISTNER, M.L.W. *A History of the Greek World, 479–323 BC.* London 1936. 3rd ed. 1957.
Text	LAMB, W.R.M. *Lysias.* London (Loeb) 1930.
Social Studies	LANG, M. *The Athenian Citizen.* Princeton, N.J. 1960.
Text	LATTIMORE, R. *The Iliad of Homer.* Chicago 1951.
Text	– *The Odyssey of Homer.* New York 1967.
Text	– *Hesiod.* Ann Arbor 1959.

Text	LATTIMORE, R. *Greek Lyrics*. 2nd ed. Chicago 1960.
Text	– *The Odes of Pindar*. Chicago 1959.
Text	LEE, H.D.P. *Plato: The Republic*. Harmondsworth 1955.
General/	
Literature	LESKY, A. *A History of Greek Literature*. Trs. James Willis and Cornelis de Heer. London 1966.
General	LÉVÊQUE, P. *The Greek Adventure*. Trs. Miriam Kochan. London 1968.
Political	LEVI, M.A. *Political power in the ancient world*. London 1965.
Historiography/	
Epigraphy	LEWIS, N. *Greek historical documents: the fifth century BC*. Toronto 1971.
Political	LINFORTH, I.M. *Solon the Athenian*. Berkeley 1919.
Science	LLOYD, G.E.R. *Early Greek Science: Thales to Aristotle*. London 1970.
Social Studies	LLOYD-JONES, H. *The justice of Zeus*. Berkeley 1971.*
General	– (ed.) *The Greeks*. London 1962.
Social Studies	MACDOWELL, D.M. *Athenian Homicide Law in the Age of the Orators*. Manchester U.P. 1963.*
Reference	MCEVEDY, C. *The Penguin Atlas of Ancient History*. Harmondsworth 1967.
Art/Architecture	MACKENDRICK, P. *The Greek Stones Speak*. London 1962.
Text	MAIDMENT, K.J. *Minor Attic Orators*, Vol. I. London (Loeb) 1941.
Crete	MARINATOS, S., HIRMER, M. *Crete and Mycenae*. London and New York 1960.
Alexander	MARSDEN, E.W. *The Campaign of Gaugamela*. Liverpool 1964.
Crete	MATZ, F. *Minoan civilisation: maturity and zenith*. Cambridge U.P. 1962 [=CAH³ Vol. II, Chs 4(b) and 12].
Economics	MICHELL, H. *The Economics of ancient Greece*. 2nd ed. Cambridge 1958.
Sparta	– *Sparta*. Cambridge 1952.
Chronology	MILLER, M. 'Solon's Timetable', *Arethusa* 1 (1968) 62–81; 'The accepted date for Solon: precise, but wrong?', *ibid.* 2 (1969) 62–86; 'Solon's Coinage', *ibid.* 4 (1971) 25–47.* *(See note at end of Bibliography.)*
Alexander	MILNS, R.D. *Alexander the Great*. London 1968.
Bronze Age	MYLONAS, G.E. *Mycenae and the Mycenaean Age*. Princeton, N.J. 1966.
Historiography	MYRES, J.L. *Herodotus, father of history*. Oxford 1953.
Religion	NILSSON, M.P. *A History of Greek Religion*. 2nd rev. ed. London 1952.
Text	NORLIN, G., VAN HOOK, L. *Isocrates*. 3 vols. London (Loeb) 1928–45.
Sparta	OLIVA, P. *Sparta and her social problems*. Amsterdam/Prague 1971.
Persia	OLMSTEAD, A.T. *History of the Persian Empire*. Chicago 1948.
Philosophy	ONIANS, R.B. *The origins of European thought about the body, the mind, the soul, the world, time and fate*. 2nd ed. C.U.P. 1953.*
Literature	PAGE, D.L. *History and the Homeric Iliad*. Berkeley 1959.*
Religion	PARKE, H.W. *Greek Oracles*. London 1967.
Art/Architecture	PATON, J.M. (ed.) *The Erechtheum*. Harvard U.P. 1927.

Crete	PENDLEBURY, J.D.S. *The Archaeology of Crete.* London 1939; repr. New York 1965.
Text	PERRIN, B. *Plutarch's Lives.* Vol. VII. London (Loeb) 1919.
Political	POPPER, K.R. *The Open Society and its Enemies.* Vol. I, *The Spell of Plato.* 3rd ed. London 1957.*
Prehistory	RENFREW, C. *The Emergence of Civilisation: The Cyclades and the Aegean in the Third Millennium B C.* London 1972.
Crete	REVERDIN, O., HOEGLER, R.E. *Crete in Colour.* London 1961.
Art	RICHTER, G.M.A. *The sculpture and sculptors of the Greeks.* 3rd ed. Oxford 1950.
Art	– *A Handbook of Greek Art.* London 1959.
Architecture	ROBERTSON, D.S. *Greek and Roman Architecture.* 2nd ed. Cambridge 1945.
Art	ROBERTSON, M. *Greek Painting.* Geneva 1959.
Text	ROGERS, B.B. *Aristophanes.* 3 vols. London (Loeb) 1924.
Text	ROLFE, J.C. *Quintus Curtius: History of Alexander.* 2 vols. London (Loeb) 1946.
Historiography	ROMILLY, J. DE *Thucydides and Athenian Imperialism.* Trs. P. Thody. Oxford 1963.
Philosophy	ROSS, W.D. *Aristotle.* 6th ed. Oxford 1955.
Science	SAMBURSKY, S. *The Physical World of the Greeks.* New York and London 1956.*
Text	SANDARS, N.K. *The Epic of Gilgamesh.* Harmondsworth 1964.
Philosophy	SCHROEDINGER, E. *Nature and the Greeks.* C.U.P. 1954.
Text	SCOTT-KILVERT, I. *Plutarch: The Rise and Fall of Athens. Nine Greek Lives.* Harmondsworth 1960.
Text	SELINCOURT, A. DE *Arrian: the campaigns of Alexander.* Rev. ed.; intro. and notes by J.R. Hamilton. Harmondsworth 1972.
Text	– *Herodotus: the Histories.* Harmondsworth 1954.
Historiography	– *The World of Herodotus.* London 1962.
Numismatics	SELTMAN, C. *Greek Coins.* 2nd ed. London 1955.
Philosophy	SHOREY, P. *What Plato Said.* Chicago 1932.
Text	SINCLAIR, T.A. *Aristotle: The Politics.* Harmondsworth 1962.
Political	– *A History of Greek Political Thought.* 2nd ed. Cleveland 1968.
Military	SNODGRASS, A.M. *Arms and Armour of the Greeks.* London and Cornell 1967.
Dark Ages	– *The Dark Age of Greece: an archaeological survey of the eleventh to the eighth centuries B C.* Edinburgh 1971.
Dark Ages	STARR, C.G. *The Origins of Greek Civilisation, 1100–650 B C.* London 1962.*
Athens, 5th c.	STE. CROIX, G.E.M. DE. *The Origins of the Peloponnesian War.* London 1972.
Bronze Age	STUBBINGS, F.H. *Chronology: the Aegean Bronze Age.* Cambridge U.P. 1962 [= CAH³ Vol. I, Ch. 6, iii].
Bronze Age	– *The rise of Mycenaean Civilisation.* Cambridge U.P. 1963 [= CAH³ Vol. II, Ch. 14].
Bronze Age	– *The expansion of Mycenaean civilisation.* Cambridge U.P. 1964 [= CAH³ Vol. II, Ch. 22(a)].
Bronze Age	– *The recession of Mycenaean civilisation.* Cambridge U.P. 1965 [= CAH³ Vol. II, Ch. 27].
Alexander	TARN, W.W. *Alexander the Great.* 2 vols. Cambridge U.P. 1948.
Bronze Age	TAYLOUR, W. *The Mycenaeans.* London 1964.

Geography	THOMSON, J. O. *History of ancient geography.* Cambridge 1948.
Topographical/ Athens	TRAVLOS, J. *Pictorial Dictionary of Ancient Athens.* London and New York 1971.
Text	TRYPANIS, C. A. (ed.) *The Penguin Book of Greek Verse.* Harmondsworth 1971.
Political	URE, P. N. *The Origin of Tyranny.* Cambridge U.P. 1922.
Reference	VAN DER HEYDEN, A. A. M., SCULLARD, H. H. *Atlas of the Classical World.* London 1959.
Bronze Age	VERMEULE, E. *Greece in the Bronze Age.* Chicago 1964.*
Text	VINCE, C. A., VINCE, J. H. *Demosthenes.* Vol. II. London (Loeb) 1926.
Text	VINCE, J. H. *Demosthenes.* Vol. I. London (Loeb) 1930.
Bronze Age	WACE, A. J. B. *Mycenae. An archaeological guide.* Princeton 1949.
Text	WARNER, R. *Thucydides: the Peloponnesian War.* Harmondsworth 1954.
Text	– *Xenophon: a History of my Times (Hellenica).* Harmondsworth 1966.
Literature	WEBSTER, T. B. L. *Greek Art and Literature 700–530 BC.* London 1959.
Literature	– *Greek Art and Literature 530–400 BC.* Oxford 1939.
Literature	– *Art and Literature in Fourth Century Athens.* London 1956.
Literature	– *Hellenistic Poetry and Art.* London 1964.
Prehistory	WEINBERG, S. S. *The Stone Age in the Aegean.* Cambridge U.P. 1965 [=CAH³ Vol. I, Ch. 10].
Text	WELLES, C. B. *Diodorus of Sicily.* Vol. VIII (Bks. XVI 66–95 and XVII). London (Loeb) 1963.
Literature	WHITMAN, C. H. *Aristophanes and the Comic Hero.* Harvard U.P. 1964.
Alexander	WILCKEN, U. *Alexander the Great.* Trs. G. C. Richards. New ed. with intro., notes and bibliogr. by E. N. Borza. New York 1967.*
Colonization	WOODCOCK, G. *The Greeks in India.* London 1966.
Colonization	WOODHEAD, A. G. *The Greeks in the West.* London 1962.
Epigraphy	– *The Study of Greek Inscriptions.* Cambridge 1959.
Historiography	– *Thucydides on the nature of power.* Harvard U.P. 1970.
Political Social Studies/	WOODHOUSE, W. J. *Solon the Liberator.* Oxford 1938.
Architecture	WYCHERLEY, R. E. *How the Greeks built Cities.* 2nd ed. London 1967.
Literature	YOUNG, D. C. *Studies in Pindaric Criticism.* London 1963.
Political	ZIMMERN, A. E. *The Greek Commonwealth: Politics and Economics in Fifth-Century Athens.* 5th ed. Oxford 1931.

Note: The date of Solon's archonship is normally given by historians as 594/3, an assumption which raises numerous historical difficulties. Numismatists, to look no further, have long argued that Athenian coinage (closely associated with Solon by our literary sources) cannot be put back beyond a date *c.* 570 BC. Lately that distinguished chronographer, Dr M. Miller, has published three meticulously argued articles (listed in the above Bibliography) placing Solon's archonship and reforms between 573 and 571. Her conclusions seem to me irrefutable, and in line with all our other testimony. I have therefore assumed their validity for the present study. Readers are entitled to know, however, that the point remains controversial.

List of illustrations

34 The sign of the double-axe incised in the north wall of the Palace at Knossos. *Photo Leonard von Matt*

35 Minoan gold double-axe, c. 1500 BC, from Arkalochori, Crete. Archaeological Museum, Heraklion. *Photo Hirmer*

36 Marble Cycladic steatopygous figure, c. 2000 BC, from Eleusis. Eleusis Museum. *Photo Edwin Smith*

37 Rock shelter of Asprochalikó, c. 40,000 BC to 13,000 BC. Courtesy Professor E. S. Higgs, Cambridge

38 Clay sealing, from 'The House of the Tiles', Lerna, c. 2200 BC. Corinth Museum. *Photo American School of Classical Studies, Athens*

39 Clay sealing with a stamp showing spider motif, from 'The House of the Tiles', Lerna, c. 2200 BC. Corinth Museum. *Photo American School of Classical Studies, Athens*

40 View from the north-west of 'The House of the Tiles', Lerna. *Photo American School of Classical Studies, Athens*

41 View of the Shaft Grave Circle and granary, Mycenae. *Photo Josephine Powell*

42 Rock-crystal dish in the form of a duck from Grave Circle B, Mycenae, c. 1600 BC. National Museum, Athens. *Photo Hirmer*

43 'Mask of Agamemnon' from Shaft Grave V, Mycenae. National Museum, Athens. *Photo Peter Clayton*

44 Mycenaean ivory pyxis lid carved from a cross-section of a tusk, from a tomb at Athens, 1400 BC. Agora Museum, Athens. *Photo Edwin Smith*

45 Seal-stone of amethyst, showing bearded head in profile, from Grave Circle B (Graves Gamma and Omicron), Mycenae, c. 1600 BC. *Photo Hirmer*

46 Heads of Mycenaean men, black niello, probably from a cup decoration, from the Palace at Englianos, near Pylos. Archaeological Museum, Heraklion. *Photo Hirmer*

47 Detail of the 'Warrior Vase' from Mycenae, c. 1200 BC. National Museum, Athens. *Photo Josephine Powell*

48 Ivory figure of a Mycenaean warrior holding a figure-of-eight shield, from Delos, 1400–1200 BC. Delos Museum. *Photo French School at Athens*

49 Upper part of a silver funnel-shaped rhyton showing Mycenaean soldiers disembarking for an assault on a town. From Mycenae, Grave IV. Archaeological Museum, Heraklion. *Photo Hirmer*

50 Aerial view of Tiryns. *Photo courtesy Rev. Professor R.V. Schoder, SJ*

51 House in Troy VIIA. *Photo courtesy the Department of Classics, University of Cincinnati*

52 Grave of young girl, Protogeometric period, c. 1000 BC. Agora Museum, Athens. *Photo Edwin Smith*

53 Detail of Geometric 'Dipylon' amphora, 750 BC. National Museum, Athens. *Photo Edwin Smith*

54 Obverse of an early Athenian tetradrachm showing the head of Athena, ?520–510 BC. British Museum, London. *Photo Peter Clayton*

55 Attic geometric oinochoe, c. 750 BC. National Museum, Athens. *Photo Deutsches Archäologisches Institut, Athens*

56 The 'Municipal Laws' of Gortyn, Crete. Text of the laws was formulated in 500 BC. *Photo Leonard von Matt*

57 Archaic ivory *kore* statuette of the Geometric period, from the Dipylon, Athens, c. 730 BC.

National Museum, Athens. *Photo Edwin Smith*

58 Wooden statuette of Hera from the Heraeum on Samos, c. 660 BC. Samos Museum. *Photo Deutsches Archäologisches Institut, Athens*

59 Bronze statuette of Apollo from Piraeus, 700–600 BC. National Museum, Athens. *Photo Edwin Smith*

60 *Kouros*, called 'Kroisos', from Anavyssos, c. 525 BC. National Museum, Athens. *Photo Hirmer*

61 Detail of krater signed by Aristonothos, showing a Greek boat, c. 660 BC. Palazzo dei Conservatori, Rome. *Photo Deutsches Archäologisches Institut, Rome*

62 Detail of krater signed by Aristonothos, c. 660 BC, showing a boat, possibly Etruscan. Palazzo dei Conservatori, Rome. *Photo Deutsches Archäologisches Institut, Rome*

63 Bronze cauldron-handle from Olympia, late 8th century BC. National Museum, Athens. *Photo Deutsches Archäologisches Institut, Athens*

64 Ivory statuette from Ephesus of a high priest. Greek work under Oriental influence, 8th–7th century BC. Archaeological Museum, Istanbul. Courtesy Deutsches Archäologisches Institut, Istanbul. *Photo W. Schiele*

65 Diagram showing griffin and young, after a bronze in Olympia Museum. Late 7th century BC. *Photo Deutsches Archäologisches Institut, Athens*

66 Cut-out bronze plaque showing griffin and young in incised detail. Probably the blazon of a wooden shield. Late 7th century BC. Olympia Museum. *Photo Deutsches Archäologisches Institut, Athens*

67 Throne with ivory inlay, sphinx and lotus motifs, showing Orientalizing influence, 7th century

BC. Cyprus Museum, Nicosia. Published by permission of the Director of Antiquities and the Cyprus Museum

68 Ivory bed from a tomb at Salamis. End of 7th century BC. Cyprus Museum, Nicosia. Published by permission of the Director of Antiquities and the Cyprus Museum

69 Ivory plaque showing sphinx, from Salamis, 7th century BC. Cyprus Museum, Nicosia. Published by permission of the Director of Antiquities and the Cyprus Museum

70 The blinding of Polyphemus. Detail from the neck of a Protoattic funerary vase, c. 650 BC. Found at Eleusis. Eleusis Museum. *Photo Deutsches Archäologisches Institut, Athens*

71 Hoplites depicted on the Chigi Vase, found at Formello, near Veii, Protocorinthian, c. 650 BC. Villa Giulia, Rome. *Photo Hirmer*

72 Marble *kouros* from Sunium, c. 600 BC. National Museum, Athens. *Photo Alison Frantz*

73 Statue of Ranofer, the Priest of Ptah of Memphis; Egyptian, Fifth Dynasty. Cairo Museum. *Photo Hirmer*

74 Coin of Lydia showing the foreparts of lion and bull. Electrum. 561–546 BC. *Photo Hirmer*

75 Boeotian statuette in terracotta showing a warrior and charioteer, 7th century BC. National Museum, Athens

76 Bronze model ploughman with ox-team, possibly a votive offering, 6th century BC. Borell Collection, British Museum, London

77 Detail of a marble relief showing an Athenian hoplite, early 5th century BC. National Museum, Athens. *Photo Deutsches Archäologisches Institut, Athens*

78 Greek armour from Argos. Possibly earliest known panoply of hoplite armour, c. 700 BC. *Photo French School at Athens*

79 Bronze of a Geometric period armourer working on helmet, 8th century BC. Metropolitan Museum of Art, N.Y.

80 Mosaic by Monnus of Hesiod, 4th century AD. Landesmuseum, Trier

81 Detail of a terracotta jug from Arkades, Crete; 7th century BC. Archaeological Museum, Heraklion

82 Perseus cuts off the head of Medusa; ivory relief from Samos, c. 630–620 BC. National Museum, Athens. *Photo Hirmer*

83 Bone-carving of a Spartan woman, c. 600 BC. Preussischer Kulturbesitz, Staatliche Museen, Berlin

84 Bone-carving of a Spartan warrior, c. 600 BC. Preussischer Kulturbesitz, Staatliche Museen, Berlin

85 Bone-carving of a Spartan warrior, c. 600 BC. Preussischer Kulturbesitz, Staatliche Museen, Berlin

86 Ivory plaque with carved warship from the Sanctuary of Artemis Orthia, Sparta, c. 600 BC. National Museum, Athens. *Photo Deutsches Archäologisches Institut, Athens*

87 Marble bust of Lycurgus, the Spartan lawgiver. Roman copy. Ny Carlsberg Glyptotek, Copenhagen

88 Herm inscribed 'Periander of Corinth, son of Cypselus; practice is everything'. Sala delle Muse, Vatican. *Photo Deutsches Archäologisches Institut, Rome*

89 Corinthian *diolkos*, built by Periander, tyrant of Corinth. *Photo Peter Clayton*

90 Area between the Acropolis and the Areopagus. *Photo American School of Classical Studies, Athens*

91 Coin of Methymna showing Arion. Reverse type, no denomination, 2nd–1st century BC. British Museum, London. *Photo Ray Gardner*

92 The 'Mnesiepean Inscription' of Archilochus on Paros. *Photo N. M. Kontoléon*

93 Detail of the inscription on the tomb of Glaucus. Found on Thasos. *Photo French School at Athens*

94 The *Partheneion* papyrus of Alcman. Louvre, Paris. *Photo Chuzeville*

95 Sappho and Alcaeus on a wine vessel by the Brygos Painter school, 480–470 BC. Staatliche Antikensammlungen, Munich. *Photo Hirmer*

96 Papyrus fragment of Sappho, 2nd century AD. Bodleian Library, Oxford

97 The 'Critios Boy', marble, c. 490–480 BC. Acropolis Museum, Athens. *Photo Hirmer*

98 Obverse of Persian coin showing the Great King with bow and arrow, c. 485–450 BC. *Photo Hirmer*

99 Detail of an amphora of Lydos, showing a mounted warrior with a squire, c. 540 BC. National Museum, Naples. *Photo Hirmer*

100 Transport of grain with mules. Detail from a black-figure cup in Attic style, 6th century BC. Louvre, Paris

101 Detail of a cup by Nikosthenes showing ploughing and sowing, from Vulci, 6th century BC. Staatliche Museen, Berlin

102 Bust of Solon. National Museum, Naples. *Photo Deutsches Archäologisches Institut, Rome*

103 Detail of an Attic black-figured amphora said to be from Agrigento, Sicily, showing men weighing merchandise; c. 550–530 BC. Metropolitan Museum of Art, N.Y.

Index